tennis
in a weekend

step-by-step techniques to improve your skills

DOMINIC BLISS

LORENZ BOOKS

This edition is published by Lorenz Books
an imprint of Anness Publishing Ltd
Blaby Road, Wigston, Leicestershire LE18 4SE
info@anness.com

www.lorenzbooks.com
www.annesspublishing.com

Anness Publishing has a new picture agency outlet for images for publishing, promotions
or advertising. Please visit our website www.practicalpictures.com for more information.

© Anness Publishing Ltd 2013

A CIP catalogue record for this book is available from the British Library.

Publisher: Joanna Lorenz
Designer: John Hawkins
Photographer: Susan Ford
Production Controller: Ben Worley

PUBLISHER'S NOTES
All instructions in this book are provided for right-handed players.

Please take care when playing tennis. The instructions offered in this book assume that the player
is in good health. It is advisable to consult your doctor before taking up any form of exercise.

Although the advice and information in this book are believed to be accurate and true at the time
of going to press, neither the authors nor the publisher can accept any legal responsibility or liability
for any errors or omissions that may have been made nor for any inaccuracies nor for any loss, harm
or injury that comes about from following instructions or advice in this book.

CONTENTS

INTRODUCTION

Tennis is a sport of extremes. It's extremely satisfying when you play good shots and win a match, and it's extremely infuriating when everything starts going wrong and you just can't seem to hit a good ball. Players at all levels experience good tennis days, when every shot seems like magic, and bad tennis days, when everything goes out of court or into the net. This book will tell you everything you need to know before you step out on court and face your first opponent, and how to eliminate the element of chance in playing an enjoyable, rewarding game.

There are many different styles of teaching and playing tennis, and therefore the instructions in this book are designed to be as basic, clear and simple as possible. But any

player who wants to reach a high level will need to consult a coach sooner or later.

Tennis is officially known as "lawn tennis" because all games were originally played on grass. Today, most people play on hard surfaces or clay, yet the basics of the game are much the same.

There are two versions of the sport: singles and doubles. Both games require a fairly high level of endurance and fitness. Singles is played on all areas of the court except the extra strips that run down the side of the court. These are called tramlines or sidelines (doubles court).

Doubles is very much a team sport where opponents do battle on the full area of the tennis court, including the tramlines (doubles court). To play doubles you do not have to be as fit as a singles player, because you will have less court to cover.

To play tennis at a beginner's level all you need are a racket, some balls, a decent pair of shoes, a tennis court and, of course, an opponent. Before you decide to get serious and join a tennis club you should try playing on a public court to get the hang of the game. If at first you don't have access to a court, you can make a start playing against a practice wall. Simply chalk a line one metre (three feet) above the ground and hit the ball back and forth against

the wall to get into the habit of hitting and responding to a ball and develop coordination.

Although tennis has the image of being a summer sport, there is no reason why you shouldn't play the game outside all year round. Whether it's hot, cold, cloudy or sunny makes very little difference to the overall game. If you really can't cope with the elements there are a large number of indoor courts to play on.

Whether you play singles or doubles, indoor or outdoor, tennis is an exciting game for all, whatever age, level of competence or degree of skill. This book offers you sound advice on improving your techniques, increasing your confidence and gaining maximum enjoyment from this popular and accessible game.

EQUIPMENT AND CLOTHING

You don't need to spend a fortune on equipment and clothing to play tennis. A racket, ball, tennis shoes and suitable clothing are all you need. However, if you want to be the most stylish player on the courts, then prepare to open your wallet!

RACKETS

Tennis rackets are the best ally a player can have; a good racket will improve the quality and enjoyment

▲ Conventional rackets are versatile.

of tennis. Rackets vary in price from the moderate to the very expensive, and the more money you invest the more likely you are to get a racket that will improve your game. If you're fairly serious about tennis then you should consider this expense as a valuable investment in your game. However, you should make sure that you are buying the correct racket for your needs.

Parts of the Racket

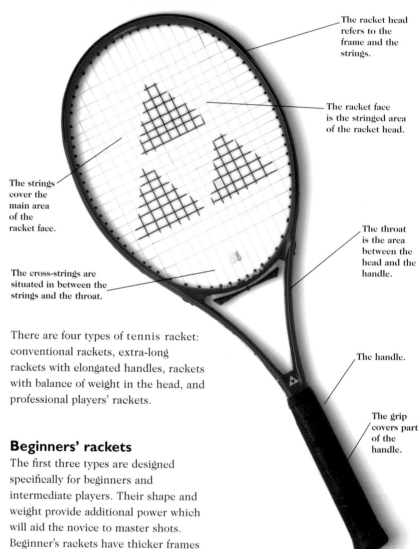

The racket head refers to the frame and the strings.

The racket face is the stringed area of the racket head.

The strings cover the main area of the racket face.

The cross-strings are situated in between the strings and the throat.

The throat is the area between the head and the handle.

The handle.

The grip covers part of the handle.

There are four types of tennis racket: conventional rackets, extra-long rackets with elongated handles, rackets with balance of weight in the head, and professional players' rackets.

Beginners' rackets
The first three types are designed specifically for beginners and intermediate players. Their shape and weight provide additional power which will aid the novice to master shots. Beginner's rackets have thicker frames and larger heads than professional rackets, and can cost more money because more material is needed to make them. Extra-long rackets give you additional height when you serve and more swing when you attempt your shots, while the rackets with balance

of weight in the head allow you to hit the ball with extra power.

Professional rackets
Professional rackets normally have thinner frames than amateur players'

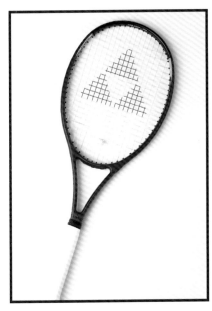

▲ Expensive rackets are a worthwhile investment if you take care of them.

rackets, because the players who use them need more control than power. For this reason they are not suitable for beginners, who need to master the basics of hitting the ball forcefully.

Children's rackets

Special junior rackets are available with smaller sized racket faces, grips and shorter handle length. However, many parents or coaches prefer to use as large a racket face as possible to save the expense of replacing it frequently, and to provide a larger hitting area, to increase the child's confidence. It is important to choose a racket with the right sized grip, so that the child's hand can hold it comfortably. A wrong-sized grip may cause injuries. A lighter-weight racket will be easier for a child to wield.

The right size

When you buy a racket you should make sure the handle is the right size or it will affect your shots and perhaps cause wrist and elbow injuries. Ideally, when you put your hand around the handle, there should be a finger's width between the ends of your little, middle and ring fingers, and your palm.

The strings

Don't underestimate the importance of a racket's strings. They are the part of the racket that connects your body with the ball and are therefore crucial. You should consider having a new racket restrung straightaway, as many factory strings are low quality and installed without much care. Most tennis coaches, club attendants or sports stores will be able to recommend a good racket stringing service.

Restringing

Most professionally-strung rackets have about 40 to 50 hours of play in them. After that the strings will become worn and your shots inaccurate. Rather than keep a tally of the number of hours you play, it is easier to remember that the number of times you play per week is the number of times you should restring your racket in a year. If you haven't used your racket for several months then you should have it restrung before you play, as the tension will slacken with time.

▲ The strings are an essential part of a racket whose maintenance is often overlooked.

◄ Re-stringing will keep your racket in good condition.

RACKETS

Tension

The tension you choose for your strings affects the power, accuracy and control of your shots. If you want power then get your racket strung at a tension of 45 to 55 pounds; if you prefer a combination of power and control, then ask for 50 to 60 pounds; and if you need more control then ask for 60 to 70 pounds. Remember that these figures are rough estimates and an experienced racket stringer will always take into consideration the head size of the racket and the materials used in the frame.

String savers

Some players like to use string savers. These are small pieces of plastic that you insert at the point where the strings cross. They prevent your strings from rubbing against one another, which wears the strings thin. They will lengthen the life of your strings, so are worth the small investment.

▲ String savers are a useful, inexpensive method of prolonging the life of your strings.

Vibration dampeners

These small, inexpensive pieces of rubber are inserted into the strings, below the bottom cross-strings, near the throat of the racket.

Vibration dampeners will prevent the racket from vibrating excessively when you strike the ball. Not only does this give you a cleaner, smoother feel when you play your shots, but it can also help prevent tennis elbow by absorbing the shock of the shot, and decreasing the pressure and harsh jarring on your joints. They will also protect your wrists from injury, an area particularly vulnerable to pain in tennis.

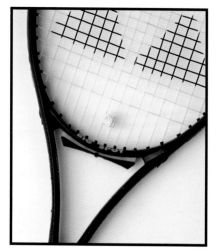

▲ Vibration dampeners absorb shock.

▲ The grip makes the racket easier to hold.

▲ Overgrips can be used to build up the racket handle to the right size for your hand.

handle of your racket is too small, then you can always build it up with overgrips. However, you should always try to buy the right size racket grip for your hand; the wrong size could be detrimental to your game.

Getting help

If you are in doubt about which racket to buy, you should consult a reputable dealer or consult your coach. The racket is the most expensive piece of tennis equipment you will buy, so you should take time and care over choosing the right one for your needs. With regular re-stringing and care, your racket should last you up to 10 years of play, so it is worth getting the right racket from the start.

▼ A good racket should last up to 10 years of regular, amateur play.

Grips

Wrapped around the handle of a racket is the grip. Just as the strings are crucial because they connect the racket with the ball, so the grip is important because it connects the racket with the player. The grip is designed to absorb sweat and to make the handle of the racket comfortable.

Types of grip

There are two types of grip: the replacement grip and the overgrip. A replacement grip is needed when the existing grip becomes worn or dirty. An overgrip is a grip wrapped on top of the existing grip and will make the grip a little bigger. If you realize that the

TENNIS BALLS

As any regular tennis player will tell you, the equipment you will buy most frequently is balls. Don't be tempted by the cheapest option. If you spend a bit of money, your tennis balls will not only last longer but they'll also make playing more enjoyable.

Types of ball

There are two types of tennis ball: pressurized and pressureless. All professionals and most amateurs use pressurized balls that come in a sealed tube with a ring-pull, even

▲ Tennis balls take a real battering and will need replacing frequently. Pressurized balls will give you more control, but will need replacing more often than the pressureless variety.

though they last much less time than pressureless balls, as they lose their firmness. However, you'll find they give you more control and "feel" when you play, because they are softer and when you hit them they will stay on the racket strings for longer. Pressureless balls are bought in a non-pressurized container and will stay firm for a longer time, but tend to give you less control over your shots because they are hard and bounce straight off the racket strings.

▲ Replace balls when they are worn or soft.

CLOTHING

Tennis shoes

The most important part of your tennis clothing is your shoes. Because tennis involves so much running around, and because it's so important that your feet grip the court surface, you'll find that a poor pair of shoes will affect your performance, wreak havoc with your feet and may encourage injury.

First, make sure that the shoe is designed specifically for tennis. Casual trainers (sneakers) or running shoes are not suitable. Second, check to see if the shoe has extra protection on the toe. Many players drag their feet when they serve, and if you play frequently you need reinforced toes or your shoes will wear out quickly.

Hard courts can cause damage to your lower legs if you play frequently

▲ Tennis shoes have special soles designed for increased grip.

for long periods of time. Therefore the heel of the shoe should be firm and supportive and the sole should have inbuilt shock absorption. Also, choose a sole pattern and material that suits the surface you intend to play on. Grass court shoes have a spiked or studded

sole; hard-court and clay-court shoes have a herringbone tread; and indoor-carpet shoes are smooth-soled. If you plan to play on a variety of surfaces, it is economical to opt for a hard-court shoe that is suitable for all surfaces. However, some indoor clubs may insist on your wearing special shoes.

▼ Most modern tennis shoes are designed for comfort and safety, with extra protection in the heel and toe to prevent damage to your feet and lower legs.

▲ Tennis shoe soles are designed to absorb shocks.

CLOTHING

▲ The classic collared shirt is still extremely popular among male and female players.

▲ Sleeveless shirts are a cooler alternative to the classic shirt.

Tennis shirts

Of course you can play tennis in any old T-shirt if you like, but a decent tennis polo shirt will not only make you look more formidable but will also improve your performance.

A lot of expensive tennis shirts are now made of special "wicking" material that draws perspiration away from the body, so you don't end up with a heavy, uncomfortable and sodden shirt after a hot five-set match. Good shirts should also include a collar to protect your neck against strong sun, and buttons or a zip on the neck to allow you to cool off or button up, depending on the weather. Nowadays the colour of the tennis shirt doesn't really matter. However, the traditional white will show sweat much less and will reflect the sun better on a hot day. Also, a number of tennis clubs, certainly the more elite ones, insist that you wear "predominantly white clothing".

Tennis shorts

A classic pair of white shorts is still the most popular choice among male players, although recently this tradition has been challenged by a number of leading tennis stars who favour cycling shorts and colourful variations of classic shorts. Tennis fashions change, and at the moment most tennis clothing companies favour extra-baggy shorts that look like pillowcases tacked around your midriff! However, this design does have its advantages. Not only do they give you freedom of movement around the court, but they are also cooler and the larger pockets mean you can keep a spare ball to hand as you are playing.

▶ Traditional shorts are usually worn by men, and increasingly by women.

Tennis skirts and dresses

Despite the fact that they can be very revealing when you play a hard shot, skirts and dresses are still a popular choice for female players. They are cooler than shorts and provide much more freedom when you run around the court. They also allow you to store your second ball in your knickers (underpants) while you serve, which is useful since some women's – and men's – hands are too small to hold two balls during the service. Classic tennis skirts or dresses are plain white but alternatives now come in many styles and colours. The classic skirt is plain white with a wrap-over panel.

▲ A traditional white tennis skirt.

The waist is elasticated for comfort. It should be a good fit: not too tight to restrict movement, but not so loose as to flap as you move around the court. Variations on the traditional skirt

▲ A variation with coloured side panels.

include panels or vents. These extra vents allow a greater freedom of movement around the court. There is also a variety of colours and patterns to choose from.

Tennis socks

Any regular tennis player will tell you that socks are a vastly undervalued tennis garment. Not only do you want socks that will absorb sweat and protect your feet from three hours of sprinting round a hard court, but you also want them to be thick enough and snug enough to provide your ankles with maximum support.

▲ Good tennis dresses combine style and fashion with practicality.

▲ Special sports socks absorb sweat well.

CLOTHING

Sweatbands

Sweatbands are small toweling bracelets worn on your wrists that allow you to wipe your forehead so that sweat doesn't run into your eyes. If you're playing in a hot climate and running around a lot, you are bound to perspire fairly heavily, so sweatbands can be a useful device for drying off without stopping to use a towel. As with other tennis clothing, there are many styles and makes to choose from.

Headbands

Headbands are useful if you have medium-length or long hair because they stop annoying strands from getting in your eyes while you are playing. They also keep sweat from running into your eyes.

Tennis bag

To keep all your tennis kit (gear) together in one place you'll need a strong bag. It should be long enough to fit a couple of rackets inside, even extra-long rackets, and compact enough to sling over your shoulder as you go out on court. Make sure it has a small pocket for your keys and money, a separate compartment for wet or dirty clothing, and a shoulder strap to help you carry it around.

Towel

A towel is useful to dry off in-between sets. Like your bag and other tennis equipment, it should be kept clear of the court for safety.

▲ Sweatbands are not essential, but many players find them invaluable in hot weather.

▲ There are many strong, lightweight sports bags on the market, which are ideal for tennis.

KNOWING THE COURT

It is important to understand the markings and layout of the court if you want to play a serious game of tennis. There are hundreds of thousands of regularly used tennis courts throughout the world, whose condition may range from pristine to potholed.

The court

The one thing that all courts have in common is their dimensions. An official tennis court should measure 23.77 metres (78 feet) long and 8.23 metres (27 feet) wide. This increases to 10.97 metres or 36 feet wide in doubles because of the extra width of the tramlines (doubles court). The material they are constructed of may be anything from clay, shale, tarmac, concrete or carpet to acrylic, artificial grass, plastic tiles, wood or grass. Each surface has its own unique playing style – some are fast, some are slow, some make the ball bounce low, some make it bounce high and some are so expensive and labour intensive to upkeep that you will find them only at the more expensive clubs and tournament venues.

The net

Get used to checking the height of the net each time before you play. Some courts will have a measuring stick available so you can set the net at exactly the right height. At the centre point it should be 0.914 metres (3 feet) above the ground; at the sides of the court it will be slightly higher. As a very rough estimate, if you place one

▲ Most tennis courts are doubles courts, adapted to the singles game.

▲ The net separates you from your opponent.

racket sideways on top of another racket placed upright, the tip of the top racket will be two or three centimetres (an inch or so) above the correct height of the net. If you are using an extra-length racket or extra-large head, then this estimate cannot be relied on.

The singles sticks

Nearly every court in the world is a doubles court (the type that has tramlines along the sides). If you are playing singles on a doubles court then officially you should support the net at both sides with singles sticks, so that passing shots down the side of the court are more difficult to play. In practice, however, very few amateur players bother doing this.

▲ Singles sticks raise the height of the net at each side of the court.

DIMENSIONS OF THE COURT

All tennis courts around the world have the same dimensions. Most courts are marked out as doubles courts, with singles sidelines (also known as tramlines) marking out the singles court. This allows you to play a doubles game or a singles game on the same court. In the singles game the doubles sidelines are considered off court.

It is useful to understand the dimensions of the court so that you can see how far you need to hit the ball and how far you need to run to achieve a particular shot. As you become more aware of the court, the more you can use it strategically to improve your shots and play to win.

The lines

On a standard doubles court, all the lines of the court should be between 2.5 cm (1 in) and 5 cm (2 in) thick, except the baseline which can be up to 10 cm (4 in) thick and the centre mark which should be 5 cm (2 in) wide and 10 cm (4 in) long.

The net

The net divides the court across the middle and should be suspended from a cord or metal cable of no more than 0.8 cm (⅓ in) in diameter. It should be attached to net posts not higher than 2.5 cm (1 in) above the top of the net cord. The net should be fully extended so that it fills up the space between the two net posts and the mesh of the net should be small enough to stop a ball passing through. It should be fairly taut, without any sag.

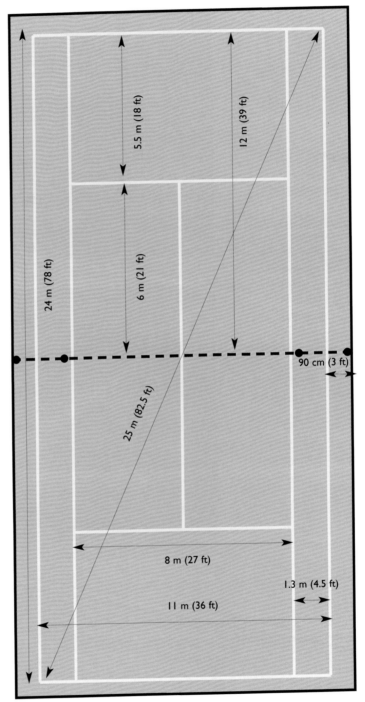

5.5 m (18 ft)

12 m (39 ft)

24 m (78 ft)

6 m (21 ft)

25 m (82.5 ft)

90 cm (3 ft)

8 m (27 ft)

1.3 m (4.5 ft)

11 m (36 ft)

PARTS OF THE COURT

At first glance the markings on a tennis court look fairly complicated, but after playing several times you will soon get used to them. The court is marked out into sections which are used for different shots. The lines and sections relate to the rules of the game; there are different areas for serving and hitting the ball.

The "horizontal" court

The court is roughly divided up into three main horizontal areas: back court, mid court and front court. The back court is bound by the baseline, the limit of the court. The centre mark marks the middle point on the baseline. The mid court is the area around the service line and the front court is the space between the net and the service line.

The "vertical" court

The court is circumscribed by the vertical lines. These are the doubles sidelines (tramlines) and the singles sidelines (tramlines). When you play singles you should ignore the doubles sidelines and treat them as though they were off court. If a ball lands in this area it is deemed out. For doubles play, the sidelines are simply treated as an extension of the court area, providing slightly more room for manoeuvre. The centre line runs through the middle of the court between the two service lines.

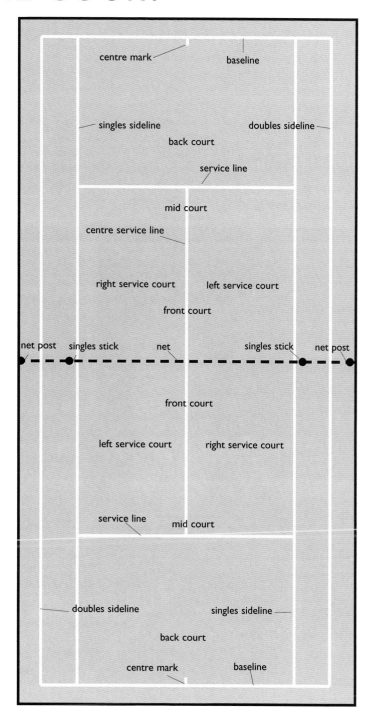

FIT FOR TENNIS

If you want to play tennis to the best of your ability you need to be fit. If you are carrying extra weight or your muscles are unused your game will suffer. Tennis is a physically demanding sport with explosive movements and fast, sometimes violent changes of direction. Therefore you need to take care to warm up, stretch and cool down properly, and to condition particular parts of your body for increased strength and agility.

WARMING UP

Stretching your muscles to warm up and cool down your body is essential for any sport. It will minimize the risk of injury during play, prevent stiffness and soreness after you play, and keep your body supple. The following exercises are the bare minimum you need to do. Do them both before and after you play, and for at least the time stated, longer if possible.

▲ Trunk rotation will increase flexibility.

Jogging

Always start your warm-up routine with a gentle jog around the court, swinging your arms at the same time. This will raise your heart beat, increase the intake of oxygen to your lungs, and warm up your major muscle groups. Jog for a minimum of five minutes, increasing your speed as you go.

▲ A jog around the court will help to prepare your body for the rigours of a hard match.

Trunk rotation

This exercise will warm up the waist area in preparation for twisting round to play forehands and backhands. Stand with your feet hip-width apart and your hands on your hips. Turn as far as possible to the left, hold for 10 seconds, then repeat on the right.

Side stretches

Stand with your feet hip-width apart, with your head looking forward and your knees slightly bent. Lift one arm straight up above your head and place the other on your hip. Gently bring your upright arm up and over your body, bending at the waist as you stretch down one side. Keep your shoulders relaxed and back and your head still looking towards the front. Don't be tempted to twist your head round in the direction of the stretch. Hold the stretch for 5 seconds and repeat on the other side.

Neck rotation

Stand with your feet hip-width apart and your eyes looking forward. Drop your head to your chest and rotate it slowly and smoothly from side to side. Don't hunch up your shoulders. This simple exercise will release tension from your neck muscles and will relax your shoulders. Repeat 10 times.

Inner thigh

Stand with your legs apart and your feet pointing forward. Keep one leg straight and bend the knee on the opposite side, transferring your weight

▲ The upright inner thigh stretch. Stretching these muscles will eliminate groin strain.

on to the bent leg until you feel a stretch in the inner thigh of your straight leg. Hold for a few seconds and repeat on the other side. This will warm up your groin muscles.

An alternative inner thigh stretch is to sit on the floor with your back straight, your head looking forward and your legs stretched out in front of you. Bring your legs as far apart as feels

comfortable without feeling any pain and, without bending or arching your back, gently lower your upper body towards the floor, walking your hands out in front of you as you lower your body. Hold for 5 seconds at the low point and repeat. If you feel any pain doing this exercise, choose the upright inner thigh stretch instead. This stretch will improve your flexibility.

WARMING UP

▲ The seated hamstring stretch. Hamstrings are used constantly in tennis.

▲ The thigh muscle stretch.

Hamstrings

Sit on the ground, stretch one leg out straight in front and tuck the opposite foot into your outstretched thigh. Lean forward, keeping your back as straight as possible, and touch your out-stretched toe. This will stretch your hamstring. Hold for 5 seconds and repeat on the other side.

Another hamstring stretch is to lie on the ground with your back flat on the floor. Bend one leg towards your body and place the foot flat on the ground. Lift the other leg straight up and clasp both hands behind your thigh. Smoothly draw the raised leg over the body. Hold the stretch for 5 seconds and repeat with the other leg.

Thigh muscle stretch

Stand with your knees slightly bent and lean on one of the net posts. Take hold of your ankle and pull it back and up towards your bottom, keeping your thighs and knees close together and your back straight. Do not pull on your ankle. Hold for 5 seconds and then repeat on the other side.

▲ The calf muscle stretch. Tennis puts a lot of strain on the muscles of the lower leg.

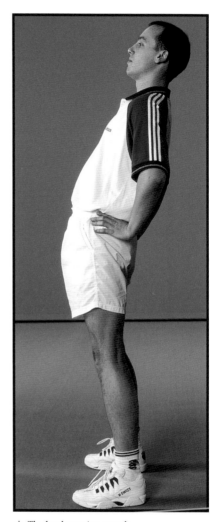

▲ The lumbar spine stretch.

Caif muscle stretch

Running around the court during a game of tennis puts pressure on your calves. Stand up and lean against the net post or a wall with your toes pointing forward. One leg should be forward and slightly bent, while the other should be back and straight. Put your weight on the forward leg and move your body forward, pressing against the net post or wall until you feel the stretch in the calf muscle of your rear leg. Make sure the heels are kept flat on the floor, especially on the straight leg, and that your back remains flat, without any arch. Hold for five seconds and then repeat the same exercise on the other leg.

Lumbar spine stretch

Stand with your hands on your hips and your feet firmly planted on the ground, hip-width apart. Slowly bend backwards with your hips pushed forward and your knees straight. Bend as far back as feels comfortable. This will help loosen up the spine area, used frequently during the serve.

WARMING UP

Tricep stretch

Stand up with your upper arm behind your head and your lower arm down behind your back. Your feet should be firmly planted on the ground, hip-width apart. Clasp your right elbow with your left hand and pull it across and down until you feel the stretch in your upper arm. Keep your head upright, with your eyes looking forward. Your back should not bend or arch. Hold for 5 seconds and then repeat on the opposite side.

Pectoral stretch

Stand up with your feet firmly planted on the ground hip-width apart. Stretch your arm out straight with your palm resting against the net post. Gently lean your upper body forward and press against the post until you feel the stretch along your arm and breast muscles. Hold for a few seconds and repeat on the other side. An alternative is to turn your head towards the net post and tilt your body slightly for an increased stretch.

Shoulder stretches

Stand with your feet hip-width apart, firmly planted on the ground. Take your arms behind your back and clasp your fingers together. Lift both arms upwards until you feel a stretch across the top of your shoulder blades. Resist the temptation to move or arch your back. Hold this stretch for 5 seconds. To stretch the front of the shoulder, take your arms in front, clasp together and round out your back, pulling forward with your arms. Hold the stretch for 5 seconds.

▲ The tricep stretch from the front.

▲ The tricep stretch from the back.

▲ The pectoral stretch.

▲ An alternative pectoral stretch.

TRAINING FOR TENNIS

Today tennis is a serious sport played by committed athletes who pride themselves on all-round fitness. Obviously amateur players don't need to be as committed as their professional counterparts, but they do need to work on their off-court fitness if they are to perform well on the court. You must always consult your doctor before doing any tough physical training and it is advisable to exercise in a supervised gym.

Weight training

The power needed for the modern game means that a lot of players need to tone up their muscles if they want to hit balls hard. After exercising and building up your muscles you will find

▲ Upper body strength is essential for both men and women if they want to hit powerful shots.

▲ Free weights are useful for training your arms, particularly your biceps.

that your on-court performance will improve considerably. You will be able to hit shots harder, jump higher for smashes, stretch further for wide shots and play more aggressively. However, weight training will only improve your fitness, it can never replace practising

your shots. Once you are confident about working with weights you can practise at home with free weights or even bags of sugar. Concentrate on building up your arm, chest, back, thigh and calf muscles, as these are used most in tennis.

TRAINING FOR TENNIS

▲ Shuttle runs will increase endurance and your responses to sudden changes of direction.

Building stamina

Because tennis is all about energetic, explosive movements around the court, it is important that you work on your sprinting to build stamina. At beginners' level, rallies can be quite long because neither player is able to hit outright winners. Therefore, you need to have enough energy to run around the court for long periods of time without resting, if you want to outplay your opponent.

Shuttle runs across the width of the court will help with this. Start on one sideline and run to the centre service line. Touch the ground, turn around and run back to the sideline where you started. Now run back across the court to the opposite singles sideline and back to your starting point. Repeat, running to the doubles sideline.

Longer runs at gentler speeds will also help build up your stamina for those tough five-set matches, as will any other aerobic form of exercise such as cycling or swimming.

Improving coordination

Playing any ball sport – such as racket ball or squash – will help your coordination. One simple way to keep your hand–eye coordination sharp is to hold the racket sideways and practise bouncing a ball up and down on the strings. Similarly, bouncing the ball up and down on the same spot – you may want to use the centre mark on the baseline as a guide – will increase your hand-eye coordination.

Another good exercise to increase hand–eye coordination is to ask someone to throw two balls at you at the same time and attempt to catch a ball in each hand. Once you have mastered this, try catching the balls with your arms crossed.

Improving balance

To practise your balance, try closing your eyes and standing on one leg with your arms outstretched for as long as you can. This will help you keep your footing around the court, as well as strengthening your ankle muscles.

▲ Bouncing the ball on the baseline will increase coordination.

▲ Bouncing the ball up and down on the racket will increase your hand–eye coordination.

INJURIES

Injuries are a fact of life for most sports people. However, you can avoid many painful experiences if you take care to warm up properly before the game, and cool down after the game. Building up your strength in particular muscles will also reduce the risk of injury.

Building wrist strength

A vigorous game of tennis will put constant pressure on your hands and wrists so it is a good idea to strengthen these muscles. Try squeezing an old, soft tennis ball 30 times a day. You'll soon feel the benifits in your grip

strength, the power of your strokes, and the length of time you can play. Also, try lifting light free weights balanced on the palms of your hands.

If you don't have any weights then a heavy plate, or bag of sugar lifted up and down in the palm of your hand will soon build up your wrist muscles.

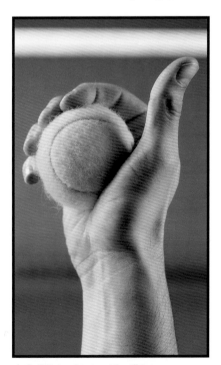

▲ Building wrist strength will improve your grip and the power of your strokes.

▲ You need strong wrists and hands to strike powerful shots.

Avoiding injury

Tennis, like any sport, can result in injuries if you are ill-prepared. If you warm up and stretch for 10-15 minutes both before and after playing, you will minimize the risk of injury. But the risk is always there. Here are some of the more common injuries you might face, with advice on what to do and how to prevent them.

Tennis elbow

Tennis elbow is the most common ailment to affect tennis players. Normally it is a slight tear or strain of the muscle attachments on the outside of the elbow. This happens because you are contracting your muscles as you grip the racket, at the same time as stretching them out as you reach the ball. Vibrations in the racket as you hit the ball can also reverberate down your arm to your elbow and cause tennis elbow. Remedies include using a lighter racket, reviewing your grip size, using vibration dampeners, or restringing your racket with less tension.

Sprained ankle

If you don't pick up the spare balls left lying around the court when playing, you run the risk of stepping on one by accident. This can be a lot more serious than it sounds, because you could sprain your ankle, which can be extremely painful and debilitating. If you do sprain your ankle, pack ice around it as soon as possible for a few minutes, and then bandage it up and seek medical help.

▲ Tennis elbow is one of the most common injuries a tennis player suffers.

▲ Accidentally stepping on a ball can be a painful experience.

INJURIES

Back injuries

If your technique or posture is not correct when you play, the stress and strain you will put on your back during serving can result in lumbar spine injuries. If you suffer from repeated back pain ask your coach what you're doing wrong. If the pain persists, consult a sports physiotherapist.

Knee injuries

Because tennis involves so much running around on hard courts and bending down for low shots, it is inevitable that knee injuries sometimes occur. If you start to feel pain you could try wearing a knee support. You may find that switching to a softer surface, such as clay or grass, will put less of a strain on your knees. If pain persists, consult a physiotherapist.

▲ Knee pain is a common complaint and can be caused by playing on hard surfaces.

▲ Back pain is another common complaint and is often caused by poor playing technique or an inadequate warm-up routine.

Calf, groin and hamstring strains

Calf strain sometimes occurs when you reach up high for a smash; groin strains happen when you stretch for a wide shot; and hamstring injuries are often caused when you suddenly sprint for a dropshot. All three need ice application and then perhaps physiotherapy. They can all be avoided with an adequate warm-up routine. Remember to cool down properly too, as sometimes you may not feel the strain until the day after your game, when it is too late to do anything about it.

Dehydration and sunburn

Because tennis is played mainly in the warm summer months, dehydration

▲ You need water to exercise properly.

▲ An injured hamstring is very painful and will put you out of action for a couple of weeks.

and sunburn and even sunstroke are dangerous risks. Dehydration occurs when you fail to replace fluids lost while sweating. In serious cases it can make you feel dizzy, tired and faint. It will certainly decrease your energy levels and detract from your game. Make sure you drink plenty of water before, during and after playing.

Lengthy exposure to the sun can result in sunburn, premature skin ageing, and even skin cancer. Make sure you wear a hat in very hot weather, and that you cover any exposed skin with sun protection cream. Children are especially prone to sunburn as their skin is more sensitive. Ensure that they are well protected with cream.

DIFFERENT GRIPS

Different tennis shots require different grips. There are five basic grips: the eastern, the semi-western, the service or "chopper", the backhand, and the double-handed backhand grip. Grip names originate from the United States where the East Coast clubs mainly had grass courts and the West Coast clubs were predominantly hard court clubs. On grass courts players required a grip that would enable them to reach the low-bouncing balls and so the eastern forehand grip developed, while on the hard courts of the West Coast they needed a grip to enable them to reach high-bouncing shots, so they adopted the semi-western and the western grips. Beginners should try to stick to the basic grips so as to achieve maximum control. Whichever grip you are using hold the racket handle firmly and make sure your hand is flexible.

▲ Assume your grip as soon as you know which shot you are about to play.

The eastern forehand grip

▲▼ Grasp the grip as though you are shaking hands with the racket, curling the thumb around. Use this to hit forehands flat or with a bit of topspin.

The semi-western forehand grip

▲▼ Use this to hit high-bouncing balls. You will find you can create a lot of topspin with this grip. Some professional players twist their hand even further around to create a full western grip. This allows them to hit the ball with even more topspin, but this is not suitable for beginners.

The backhand grip

▲▼ This is suitable for players who hit their backhands with just one hand. You achieve it by twisting your hand slightly around to the left. It is simple to do but beginners should be encouraged to switch to the more conventional double-handed grip.

The service or "chopper" grip

▲▼ Hold the racket as if it were an axe (hence the name "chopper"). Beginners may prefer to start serving with an eastern forehand grip, but this should be modified to a chopper grip as confidence grows. It is hard to get the required power, speed or accuracy in your service if you don't learn to use the "chopper" grip.

The double-handed backhand grip

▲▼ Place your leading hand in the backhand grip position and your second hand above it and touching it in the forehand position. You'll have less reach than you do with a single-handed backhand grip, but you'll have more strength in your shots. With this grip you'll find that you can disguise from your opponent whether you plan to hit the ball down the line or across court.

THE SERVE

Serving is probably the most crucial part of the modern game and the area that gives beginners the most trouble. When tennis first started over a century ago, the service was supposed to be a fair and equal start to a rally. Today a player's service can make or break a match. If you don't have a strong serve you are unlikely to win the game.

Since you have two chances to make a good serve, you should try to hit your first serve with power and pace, and your second serve slightly more slowly in order to guarantee that it goes in. Don't risk a double fault; it will destroy your confidence and give your opponent a free point.

In singles you should stand near the centre of the baseline after serving, so that you can control the whole court or, if you are a serve-and-volleyer, you will need to run straight forward to the centre of the net.

Keep your arm straight and toss the ball in the air above your head and slightly to the racket side of your body.

Keep your eyes on the ball at all times. Try not to lower your head too soon or you'll find the ball will go into the net.

PERFECT POSTURE

The first serve is all about power and accuracy. Try to throw your racket arm at the ball with lots of force and stretch your body up straight to get as much height as possible. Remember the higher you are, the more you will see of the service box on the other side of the net when you are behind your own baseline.

As you throw the ball up your racket should be down behind your back so that you can whip it up and over the ball and create as much power as possible.

Your body should be at full stretch when you strike the ball generating as much height as possible.

Legs should be slightly apart.

Make sure your feet don't touch the baseline or the interior of the court before you strike the ball. This will constitute a fault.

Stand at a 45-degree angle to the baseline.

THE FIRST SERVICE

The first service is played at the beginning of a point.

The serve is the only shot in tennis over which you have total control. Other shots are responses to your opponent's shots. It is also a shot which can pick you up points quickly.

Remember that you have two chances to serve. For the first serve try to generate as much power as you can. You can play a safer shot on the second service if the first service is out.

Aim to hit the ball to either of the two furthest corners of your opponent's service box, forcing him to run wide to the side of the court or into the middle of the court, leaving him vulnerable for your return shot. If you can vary your serves both to the left and the right service box, you will keep your opponent on his toes and break any strategies or rhythm he has developed.

Once you have delivered the shot you should either get ready to return to your baseline or attack the net and volley the return.

1 Stand at a 45-degree angle to the baseline with your legs slightly apart and your front foot about five centimetres – or about two inches – behind the baseline.

2 Lower the racket and the ball together to just below your thigh area. Keep your eyes focused on the service box that you are aiming for – left or right.

Grips ▶

At first you will find it tricky and unnatural, but you must try to use the service or "chopper" grip, as it is known.

Beginners may like to start by using the eastern forehand grip for serving, but they should progress to the service grip when they have gained confidence. As you strike the ball your wrist should snap downward so that the ball doesn't land beyond the service box. If you don't progress beyond using the forehand grip, your serves will always be flat. This means your shots will lack power and will be easier to return.

"Chopper" grip

Eastern forehand grip

3 Lift up the ball and place it in the air a few feet above your head and slightly in front and to the racket side of your body. At the same time move your racket down.

4 Bring the racket head up, behind the back of your head, and down your back. It should feel as though you are scratching your back with the racket.

5 Smoothly bring the racket forward and strike the ball slightly in front of you when your body is at full stretch.

Practice

The service is the most infuriating shot in tennis because if you start serving badly in a match it can ruin your concentration and throw the rest of your game. You must practise your service technique frequently. Go regularly to your local tennis court and repeatedly serve hundreds of balls. There is no short cut to perfecting your serve. You have got to work at it.

Avoid slipping ▶

The grips of your shoes sometimes get clogged up with dirt, especially if you play frequently on clay or grass courts. Before you serve it is a good idea to clear this dirt by banging your soles lightly with your racket. This will stop you from slipping as you sprint off after the serve. If you play regularly it may be worth buying a pair of tennis shoes with soles specially designed for clay or grass courts. Although hard court shoes are perfectly adequate for all surfaces their moulded soles may cause clogging on soft surfaces, especially in damp or wet weather.

THE FIRST SERVICE

Serving aces

An ace is a serve that lands in the correct service box and is not touched by the receiver. It is perhaps the most satisfying, dynamic and exciting shot in tennis, because you win the point outright and your opponent is left flustered. You will feel psychologically stronger after hitting an ace as there is no come-back.

The ace is a difficult shot to achieve because there is not much room for error, so don't rely on it. It is usually achieved on the first service, as the second service is usually a safer, less powerful shot.

6 Follow through in the direction of the ball, curling your wrist slightly forward so that the ball doesn't land way beyond the service box.

7 Bring the racket head down and to the other side of your body and then immediately get ready to play the next shot.

Short players

When it comes to serving, short players are at a disadvantage.

Imagine that there is a line from where your racket strikes the ball to your opponent's service box. If you are tall this line will be straight. If you are short this line will have to loop slightly upwards and then down again. Short players have to jump as they serve or put topspin on the ball to loop it over the net.

Position and posture ▶

When you are serving, make sure you keep your head raised as you strike the ball. If you lower your head too soon your arm and upper body will automatically be lowered and you'll find that the ball goes into the net. You will also not be able to see immediately where the ball has landed, and respond quickly to the returned shot.

You need to position yourself for the return immediately. If you are a serve-and-volleyer, you need to be already on your way to the net immediately after you have completed your serve. It may come back just as fast. If you favour baseline play, then you need to be behind the baseline in the middle, ready for your opponent's return.

THE SECOND SERVICE

The second serve is played if your first service is out. It is your second chance at the point.

Don't worry if you don't get your first serve in. You should be hitting it with a lot of power and there is always the risk of putting it long or into the net. You cannot afford to take any risks on your second service. There is nothing worse than a double fault to ruin your concentration, give away an easy point and make you feel psychologically weaker than your opponent.

A good dependable second service is one where your racket comes up and round the outside of the ball. This will put topspin on the ball and cause it to loop over the net positioned well inside the service box.

However, the second serve should not necessarily mean a slower or weaker serve, it should merely be a different type of shot. Topspin will slow down the speed of the ball and control its direction, so that it gently loops over the net.

1 Stand at a 45-degree angle to the baseline with your legs slightly apart. You should be facing a little bit more to the side than you did for the first service.

2 Lower the racket and the ball together to around thigh height. Keep your eyes focused on the service box that you are aiming for – either left or right.

Grips ▶

You should use the "chopper" or service grip for the second serve. (Beginners may prefer to start serving with an eastern forehand grip, but this should only be used temporarily.)

◀ Bouncing the ball

Many players bounce the ball on the ground several times before they serve to improve their concentration. It will also develop your hand–eye coordination skills.

"Chopper" grip

THE SECOND SERVICE

3 Lift up the ball and place it in the air a few feet above your head and slightly in front and to the racket side of your body. At the same time move your racket down.

4 Bring the racket head up and behind the back of your head, into the "back scratch" position.

5 Bring the racket up and round the outside of the ball as you hit it, putting some spin on to the ball. This will loop it over the net and down into the service box.

In or out?

Serving is the hardest time to tell if the ball is in or out because most serves land on or close to the service line. If the ball is out, call "out" immediately, before you hit your return shot. If you are unsure, then ask to play a let which means the point is replayed. Remember, if you play a let on a second service you must return to the first service and replay the whole point again.

◄ Aiming for power

Practise lowering the racket down behind your back as you serve. This will allow you to "throw" the racket head at the ball and generate as much speed and power as possible. If you start "throwing" the racket head from a higher position you will not get as much speed and power because the racket will be closer to the ball and there will be no whipping action.

Practise your throw ►

Practise the ball toss by placing your racket on the floor in front and to the right and throwing the ball up in the air to land on the stringbed of the racket. Make sure you extend your arm fully before you release the ball. If the ball lands on the racket strings then you know you are throwing the ball up correctly.

6 Follow through with the racket on the outside of the ball, making sure that it curls up and over the net right into the service box.

7 Bring the racket head down to around knee height and over to the other side of your body. Immediately get ready to play the next shot either at the baseline or the net.

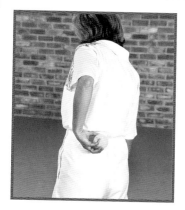

Holding the ball

Some players find it hard to hold two balls in their hand when they serve. If your skirt or shorts don't have a big enough pocket to accommodate the second ball, then you can either tuck it into your knickers (underpants) or buy a ball clip which attaches to the back of your skirt or shorts.

Aim

Remember this is your second serve, and your last chance, and you must be sure to get the ball in. Try to aim for the ball to loop over the net so that it is guaranteed to land in the service box.

Topspin will give you more control over the aim and speed of the ball. Vary the amount you use according to the situation.

Return position

The safest position to prepare for your opponent's return of serve is by standing behind the centre of the baseline. Very few players will even contemplate playing serve-and-volley tactics on a second serve, because second serves are generally weaker than other shots, and will probably be pounded back over the net by the opponent.

THE UNDERARM SERVICE

The underarm serve is a very rare shot and should only be used in emergencies, usually on the second service, your last chance at the point.

Sometimes your serving will go horribly wrong. It happens to everybody, even the top players. Occasionally you will have to resort to a fail-safe serve.

If, in exceptional circumstances, you do decide to do this then keep the ball low and try to put as much backspin on the ball as possible. This means that your opponent is not only caught unawares, but has to run forward quickly to reach the serve before it bounces twice.

Contrary to popular belief, it is not illegal in tennis to switch suddenly to an underarm serve without warning your opponent.

1 Assume the receiving position at a 45-degree angle to the baseline. Hold the ball on the string-bed of the racket.

2 Take your racket back half-way around your body and throw the ball lightly into the air at about the level of your shoulder. Don't toss the ball high into the air.

Getting closer to the net

In any of the three serves – first, second or underarm – you are permitted to leap across the baseline before you hit the ball as long as your feet remain in the air before the ball is struck. Many serve-and-volleyers do this so that they get that extra few inches closer to the net and are in a better position for the volley.

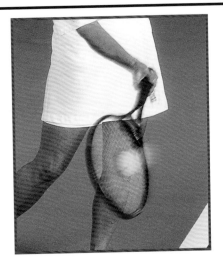

◀ **Backspin**

To achieve backspin on a ball you should bring the racket below the ball and lift it up using a slicing motion, aiming to send it over the net. Backspin will cause the ball to bounce short and low forcing your opponent to sprint forward to return it.

Grip ▶

For the underarm serve you should use the service or "chopper" grip, so that you can put as much backspin as possible on the ball.

When to use the underarm serve

The underarm serve is useful if you are playing outside on a very windy day as the throw-up is so short that a strong gust of wind is less likely to blow the ball away.

It can also be used if the sun is shining brightly into your eyes when you throw the ball up. Bright sunlight will dazzle you for several seconds and you won't be able to focus on the ball when it's in the air. Likewise, when it's raining you'll avoid getting raindrops in your eyes.

3 Strike the ball to the right and slightly in front of your body. Slice the racket under the ball so as to impart maximum backspin which will control the ball.

4 Follow right through the shot, bringing your arms to roughly shoulder height. Catch your racket on the other side of your body with your non-playing hand.

"Chopper" grip

Avoiding foot faults ▶

In all three types of serve – first, second and underarm make sure you don't touch the baseline or the area within the boundary of the court with your foot before you strike the ball. This constitutes a foot fault and therefore a foul serve. A lot of amateur players ignore this rule and wonder why they are penalized when they come to play competitive matches.

Even professional players occasionally make this mistake and it can make a big difference to the score over the course of a whole match.

However, you are permitted to leap up into the air during the shot, landing over the baseline as you descend, as long as you do not land before you hit the ball. Your feet must be in the air while the ball is struck. See "Getting Closer to the Net", opposite.

GROUNDSTROKES

Groundstrokes are the bread and butter of any rally in tennis and you will find that you play more of these than any other shot. They include all shots played on the forehand and backhand after the ball has bounced once. Make sure you master them so that you can sustain a good rally with your opponent.

You should learn to have confidence in your groundstrokes and rely on them. They are probably the easiest shots to play and, because they are the backbone of your repertoire, you should work hard at perfecting them.

The vast majority of beginners will find that their forehand groundstrokes are much stronger than their backhand. Work hard on your backhand too, because if opponents realize you have a weaker side they will inevitably try to exploit it.

PERFECT POSTURE

Groundstrokes, as their name suggests, are usually played closer to the ground than other shots such as the serve, which depends on power and height.

You should keep your knees bent, ready to sprint off quickly to respond to a shot, and your free hand should be used to maintain your balance and offer an anchor against the force of a powerful return. Similarly, your feet should be firm on the ground, to steady your body.

Remember to keep your head upright and focused on the ball so you can keep alert to returned shots.

Keep your eyes on the ball at all times. This will stop you mis-hitting.

Your grip should be firm but flexible.

Use your non-playing hand to maintain your body's balance.

Your knees should be slightly bent.

You should make little steps until you are in the right position to hit the ball.

Your feet should be firmly on the ground so your body remains in a solid position throughout the shot.

45

THE FLAT OR TOPSPIN FOREHAND

A forehand shot is when a player hits the ball that is on the right side of his body, if he is right-handed, and on the left-hand side of his body if he is left-handed. It is the most natural stroke for a player to make.

The flat or topspin forehand should be a failsafe stroke and one that regularly produces winning shots. If you are able to hit your forehands with topspin (i.e. up, over and through the direction of the ball) you will find that you can hit the ball much harder and it will still land inside the court.

Forehands can be useful for sending the ball diagonally across the court and straight down the line.

You should aim to develop your forehand to such an extent that you can vary where you put the ball and keep your opponent guessing.

1 Assume the ready position, standing well behind the baseline, with your knees bent and head looking forward watching the progress of the ball.

2 Release your non-playing hand from the racket and start taking it back as soon as you know whether the ball is coming to your forehand or backhand side.

Practice

You should practise hitting your topspin forehands both diagonally across the courts and straight down the line. Always keep your opponent guessing as to where you are going to place the ball. If you master topspin you will find that you can hit the ball very hard without causing it to land way beyond the baseline of your opponent's court.

Eastern forehand grip

Semi-western grip

3 Take the racket right back behind you in a smooth semi-circle so that you can hit the ball with maximum swing. Start stepping forward, transferring your weight.

4 Keeping your eyes fixed on the flight of the ball, step forward towards it with your leading foot and swing the racket head at it. Lift the racket from low to high.

5 Follow up, over and then through the direction of the ball, so as to give the ball topspin, controlling its speed and where it will land.

◀ Grips

Beginners should hit the forehand with the eastern forehand grip. Pretend you are shaking hands with the racket. When you have mastered this shot you may want to start using the semi-western grip so as to impart more topspin onto the ball.

Posture ▶

Make sure you don't hunch up your body too much when you play your groundstrokes. Give yourself room between your body and the ball in order to swing your racket properly. Ideally, you should strike the ball slightly in front of you with your arm slightly bent.

Forehand slice

Some players like to use a forehand slice. This is when the player brings the racket head underneath the ball to put backspin on it, rather than up and over the ball, creating topspin.

Although this can be an effective shot, especially on slow surfaces like clay and shale, it is not very common and is tricky to master.

THE FLAT OR TOPSPIN FOREHAND

The right foot

Make sure you don't hit the ball with the wrong foot forward or you risk losing control. You should have your left foot forward when you play a forehand (right foot if you are left-handed) and your right foot forward when you play a backhand (left foot if you are left-handed).

6 Bring the racket right round to the other side of your body. The racket face should be slightly closed, i.e. pointing downwards towards the ground.

7 A full follow-through means the ball will stay on the strings of your racket for as long as possible which will give you more control over where the ball lands.

Hitting the ball ▶

If you don't get to the ball in time, you are not allowed to throw your racket at the ball in the hope that you will hit it and send the ball back. You must be holding the racket when you hit the ball for it to be a legal shot.

You should aim to hit the ball an arm's length away from your body, slightly in front of you, just as it reaches the top of its bounce. Use your other hand to maintain balance.

THE FLAT OR TOPSPIN BACKHAND

A backhand is a shot hit by a player on the left-hand side of the body, if right-handed, and on the right-hand side of the body if left-handed.

Most players, particularly beginners, are weaker at playing backhands than they are at playing forehands. Your opponent will know this and may try to put pressure on you by continually playing to your backhand side. You should be confident in your backhand and practise it until it is solid.

Don't get into the habit of running around the ball so as to turn a backhand shot into a forehand one. Your opponent will realize what you are doing and turn it against you. You will not be able to respond to shots adequately either.

As with the forehand, you should practise hitting your backhands both diagonally and straight down the line to keep your opponent guessing as to where you are going to place the ball.

1 Always start in the ready position, behind the baseline, with your knees slightly bent and your head forward, with your eyes on the ball.

2 Start taking your racket back as soon as you know whether the ball is coming to your forehand or backhand side. Release your non-playing hand from the racket.

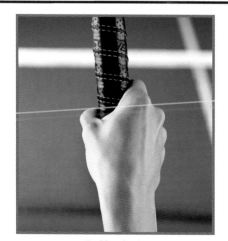

Backhand grip

◀ Grip
You should use the backhand grip when you play the flat or topspin backhand.

The right distance ▶
If, on the backhand, you stand too close to the ball as you hit it, you risk scraping your knee with your elbow as you swing through with the racket. This will cause you to mis-hit the ball.

THE FLAT OR TOPSPIN BACKHAND

3 Take the racket right back behind you so that you can hit the ball with a lot of swing. Start stepping forward with your leading foot.

4 Keeping your eyes fixed on the flight of the ball step forward towards it with your leading foot and swing the racket head at it. Lift the racket from low to high.

5 Follow up, over and then through the direction of the ball so as to give it a powerful topspin.

A strong backhand

It's important to get over the psychological barrier the backhand sometimes presents. The best way to develop this stroke is to practise hard. It can be a formidable shot if executed with power and accuracy. If your opponent continually exploits your weakness on this stroke, simply watch and learn. You will soon improve.

◀ **Strengthen your wrists**
To exercise your wrist for the backhand, squeeze an old, soft tennis ball in each of your fists repeatedly to build up strength. If you do this exercise 30 times a day, you will soon notice a difference in the power of your backhand strokes.

Building up your arm and shoulder strength with weights may also help improve this shot.

THE DOUBLE-HANDED BACKHAND

The double-handed backhand stroke is similar to the ordinary backhand, but uses two arms to hold the racket instead of one.

This stroke was originally developed for female players, smaller male players, or children who found that they couldn't generate enough power on the backhand side. By using two arms instead of one, they were able to create a lot more force and hit the ball much harder. Today, even strong players might use the double-handed backhand stroke because it is such a powerful shot.

The main disadvantage to the double-handed backhand is that you will find you are not able to reach as far as you can with a single-handed backhand. You will have less reach, but you'll have more strength in your shots.

You will also have to recover much faster, and run and react more quickly in order to get into a receiving position in time to anticipate and return the on-coming ball.

1 Always start in the ready position, behind the baseline, with knees bent and your eyes on the ball. Grip the racket firmly with both hands.

2 Start taking your racket back as soon as you realize the ball is coming to your backhand side. Swivel your grip so that your correct hand is in the backhand grip.

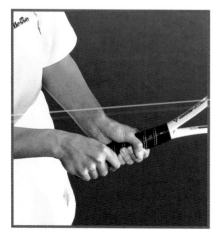

Double-handed backhand grip

◄ Grip

Use the double-handed backhand grip. Place your leading hand in the backhand grip position and your second hand above it and touching it in the forehand position.

This is a powerful grip as you will have the whole weight of your body behind it.

The right distance from the ball ►

If you wait too long to return the ball on a double-handed backhand and it comes in too close to your body, you risk scraping your knee with your elbow and mis-hitting the ball. Remember that it is the middle of the racket face which should make contact with the ball.

THE DOUBLE-HANDED BACKHAND

3 Take the racket right back behind you so that you can hit the ball with a large, powerful swing.

4 Start stepping forward with your leading foot as the ball approaches. Don't wait too long to respond to the ball.

5 Keeping your eyes fixed on the ball, step forward towards it with your leading foot and swing the racket head at it. Lift the racket from low to high.

◄ The right foot

Make sure you don't hit the ball with the wrong foot forward or you'll lose control of the shot. You should have your leading right foot forward when you play a backhand (or your left foot if you are left-handed).

Position ►

Don't plant yourself too far away from the ball or you'll have to stretch in order to reach it and you won't be able to strike it properly. You will need to position yourself slightly closer to the ball than you would be for the single-handed backhand because your doubled-handed grip will have less reach. For this shot, it is even more important than usual to get yourself in the correct position before swinging the ball.

6 Follow right through and over the ball so as to give it some topspin.

7 Your follow-through should finish with the racket right behind your opposite shoulder so that the ball stays on the strings of the racket for as long as possible.

Give yourself room

Don't hunch up your body when you play the double-handed backhand or you won't be able to swing your racket to its full extent.

Leading foot forward

Both on the forehand and the backhand, practise striking the ball with your leading foot forward. Your leading foot is always the opposite foot to the side of the body on which you are playing the ball. If you practise enough, the correct foot position will eventually become second nature.

THE BACKHAND SLICE

The backhand slice is a shot where you draw the racket across the body as with the ordinary backhand, and you bring the racket head slightly underneath the ball.

Sometimes the ball will bounce very low, too low for you to be able to hit a flat or topspin backhand. At times like this you should hit a backhand slice. This shot has very little power, but it can be extremely effective.

You should aim to keep the ball as low as possible over the net and put a lot of backspin on it, so that when it lands in your opponent's court it bounces very short and low.

The backhand slice will force your opponent to play a defensive shot. The ball will remain very low on the ground and he will have to slice the ball rather than play an attacking topspin shot back to you.

It is important to learn how to impart slice; it is useful for both forehand and backhand strokes.

1 Assume the ready position, behind the baseline and start taking the racket back as soon as you realize the ball is coming to your backhand side.

2 Take the racket right back behind you so that you can hit the ball with a lot of swing. Start stepping forward with your leading foot.

"Chopper" grip

◄ Grip

For the backhand slice use the (one-handed) "chopper" or service grip.

Avoid the net ►

When you play a forehand or backhand slice, try to avoid playing the ball with the racket too closed (too vertical) or the ball will just fly into the net.

3 Keeping your eye on the ball, step forward with your leading foot and swing the racket head at it. Bring the racket head slightly underneath the ball so as to slice it.

4 Follow under and through the direction of the ball so as to maximize the slice. The more slice you give the ball, the slower it will travel through the air.

5 A full follow-through means the ball will stay on the strings of your racket for as long as possible and you will be able to control its direction much better.

◄ **Perfect posture**

When playing a forehand or backhand slice, make sure you don't hunch up your body too much when you play the slice. Give yourself room between your body and the ball or you won't be able to swing your racket properly.

The right height ►

Don't play a slice with the racket face too open (too horizontal) or the ball will go high up into the air. This applies to both forehand and backhand slice.

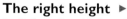

THE VOLLEY

The volley is crucial. In doubles, the team that controls the net is always the team that wins the match. In singles, especially on fast surfaces such as hard courts or grass, the winner is quite often the one who is the more dominant at the net.

Many advanced players will try to reach the net any time they can. If they don't use serve-and-volley tactics and storm the net immediately after serving, then they might wait until they play a really strong shot from the baseline. This will put their opponent on the defensive, and they might be able to use that opportunity to run to the net and, hopefully, kill the ball with a volley.

Even if you become a predominantly baseline singles player, you should still be able to put away a good volley when the occasion arises.

Keep your eyes focused on the approaching ball.

Keep the head of the racket up so that you don't play the ball into the net.

Your grip should be firm, but flexible.

Use your non-playing hand to maintain your body's balance.

Always keep your knees bent when playing a volley.

PERFECT POSTURE

For the volley, stand about two metres (six feet) from the net. As soon as you know which side of your body the ball is coming to, bring up the head of the racket and bend your knees in preparation for hitting the ball. The shot should be a punching motion with a firm grip and, unlike groundstrokes, there should only be a very short follow-through.

THE FOREHAND VOLLEY

A volley is when you hit the ball before it bounces on the ground. It should be a sharp, punching motion with a short follow-through and a firm grip. Most volleys are played close to the net.

It is much easier to play a winning shot with a volley than with a groundstroke. Volleys are played much closer to the net, normally about two metres (six feet) and they give your opponent less time to return the ball. If you hit a volley correctly you can put the ball away with much more power and accuracy than if you are playing a backhand or forehand groundstroke from the back of the court.

Aim to hit the volley low and deep so that it lands just inside the baseline at a very shallow angle. This will make it very difficult for your opponent to return the ball effectively. You should be able to ride the next shot that comes to you if your first volley is strong and deep.

1 Start in the ready position. For doubles you'll need to be covering your side of the net. For singles you'll need to be in the middle of the court, ready to go either way.

2 Start transferring the weight of your body on to your leading foot (your left foot, if you're right-handed, or your right foot if you're left-handed).

Where to stand

For the volley you should stand about two metres (six feet) from the net. This will give you enough reaction time and enough room to manoeuvre.

If you are too close to the net you won't have time to react or you might clip the net with your racket. If you are too far away from the net, you risk putting the ball into, rather than over, the net.

"Chopper" grip

◄ Grip

For both the forehand and the backhand volley use the "chopper" or service grip. This will enable you to put a bit of slice on the ball and prevent it from landing outside the back of your opponent's court.

Posture ►

Make sure you really bend your knees, especially when the volley is coming in low. This will prevent you from putting the ball into the net.

3 Start moving as soon as you know which side the ball is coming to. Take only a short backswing and keep your eyes on the ball at all times.

4 Bend your knees and non-racket arm slightly, and try to make contact with the ball, level with your leading foot, a comfortable distance away from your body.

5 Your weight should now be on the left foot (or right foot if you are left-handed). The shot should be a punching motion with a firm grip and a short follow-through.

Tactics

If you are a serve-and-volley player who storms the net immediately after a serve, your opponent will try to return your serve right to your feet as you run in close to the net.

Experienced players can volley these low balls just above the ground and put them back over the net very low. This takes a lot of practice but is well worth the effort.

THE FOREHAND VOLLEY

Position

The ideal position for the volley, when playing singles, is to be placed slightly towards the back of the service box in the middle of the court. This will give yourself maximum reaction time and enough room to manoeuvre. For doubles you need to be covering your side of the net.

Try to play your volley as far away from your opponent as possible, but without risking putting the ball out. Generally, volleys played deep towards the corner of the opposite baseline are more effective, because they will bounce low and give your opponent less room to manoeuvre.

6 Get straight back into the ready position as soon as you have played the shot, so that you're ready for the next one.

7 Remember that next time you'll have much less reaction time if you are closer to the net, because you are also closer to your opponent.

◄ Clipping the net

Be sure not to clip the net with your racket as you play a volley because this constitutes a foul shot. Similarly, if any part of your hand, body or clothing touches the net while the ball is still in play, this is also a foul shot. But if you play a good volley and the ball bounces twice or more before you clip the net, then it is not a foul shot.

THE BACKHAND VOLLEY

The backhand volley is just like the forehand volley, but on the other side of your body, with the racket drawn across the body and over the opposite shoulder. Similarly, it is a punching motion with a short follow-through and a firm grip.

When receiving or responding with a backhand volley, you should aim to stand about two metres (six feet) from the net. This means you will be far enough away to allow yourself reaction time before the ball reaches you. But at the same time, you'll be close enough to the net so that you cut down the angle of your opponent's shot, rather like a goalkeeper in soccer who runs towards a striker in order to cut down the angle of a shot at goal.

If your volley is not very strong on the backhand side, try to prevent your opponent discovering this, or he will repeatedly send the ball past you on your weaker side.

1 Assume the ready position with knees slightly bent and firm grip. Ideally, you should be in the middle of the court, ready to go whichever way the ball comes at you.

2 Be ready to cover both sides of your body. Prepare yourself as early as possible, but take only a short backswing.

"Chopper" grip

◀ Grip

For backhand volley use the "chopper" or service grip. You will then be able to impart a bit of slice on the ball and stop it from landing outside the back of your opponent's court.

Dangerous volleys

The hardest volleys to play – whether backhand or forehand – are ones that come in low and straight towards your body. For these you will have to have lightning reactions. Move your body to the side and get the racket in the path of the ball. But take care; if you don't move fast enough, you may get hit by the ball.

THE BACKHAND VOLLEY

3 Start transferring the weight of your body on to your leading foot. Keep your eyes on the approaching ball at all times.

4 With your knees and arm bent, make contact with the ball level with your leading foot, a comfortable distance away from your body.

5 Transfer your weight on to your right foot (or left foot if you are left-handed). The shot should be a punching motion with a firm grip.

◄ Aim

Try to punch the ball with the racket as you hit it. Remember always to keep the head of the racket above your wrist so that the ball doesn't go into the net. If you have to take the ball really low below the top of the net, then your racket face should be open so that your ball goes upward and over the net. Your wrist should be firm. As your volleying improves, you'll find that you're able to direct the ball so that it lands far away from your opponent.

Net position

Positioning yourself at the net is a powerful tactic. Your opponent will feel intimidated because you are so close. He will be faced with only two choices because he wants at all costs to avoid playing the ball to you. He can either play a very fast and low passing shot down either side of the court (which is hard to do) or lob the ball above your head which might risk giving you the opportunity for a smash. You should therefore make the most of your position at the net and aim to keep it until the point is decided.

6 There should be only a short follow-through with the racket.

7 Get straight back into the ready position as soon as you have played the shot, so that you're prepared for the next one.

◄ Placing the ball

It is important to make sure the face of the racket is not too open (i.e. pointing upwards towards the sky) or the ball will go high into the air and possibly out of the back of your opponent's court.

Make sure that you are not so close to the net that you accidentally hit the ball before it has passed the line of the net. This would constitute a foul shot. The ball must be on your side of the net when you hit it.

OTHER
IMPORTANT SHOTS

The great thing about tennis is that you never know what kind of shot you're going to have to play next. Although the majority of shots are serves, groundstrokes or volleys, sooner or later you'll have to learn to do more unusual shots such as lobs, smashes and dropshots.

It's essential you learn how to do these shots so that you can use them when the occasion calls, and so that you can keep your opponents guessing as to which shot you are about to play. The player who always plays the same shots soon becomes very predictable and easy to beat.

PERFECT POSTURE

In this section you will learn how to tackle valuable, yet less orthodox shots like lobs, dropshots and smashes.

Here is a forehand smash. Like the serve, it is a powerful stroke which reaches high into the air, favouring the taller player. The racket is drawn as far back behind the back as possible, producing a forceful stroke with the whole force of your body behind it.

Always point at the falling ball with your free hand. This will make your smash more accurate.

Keep your eyes on the ball at all times.

Take the racket right down behind your back so that you can hit the ball with maximum power.

Hit the ball at full stretch so that you have maximum height.

Position yourself under the ball with short, little sideways steps.

THE FOREHAND LOB

The lob is when you send a low ball up high, aiming the ball over your opponent's head. A lob can be very effective against a shorter player, but it is dangerous to lob a very tall player because they will find it easy to return the ball with a smash, a powerful and dangerous shot.

The lob is best used when your opponent is at the net. When he is in this position you have two choices. Either try to hit a passing shot – i.e. a normal groundstroke hit fast and to one side of your opponent – or try a lob, sending the ball high over his head, well out of his reach.

These instructions describe how to play a lob on the forehand side. To play a lob on the backhand side, the technique is exactly the same.

1 Always start in the ready position. There's no point lobbing unless your opponent is at the net and you are trying to put the ball over his head.

2 Start taking the racket back as soon as you know whether the ball is coming to your forehand or backhand side.

Practice

Because the lob is an unusual shot, you will rarely get the chance to practise it during normal play. Therefore when you are just practising and playing basic groundstrokes, occasionally try hitting a lob so that you get a feel for it and it becomes a natural shot to play, and another useful stroke in your repertoire.

Eastern forehand grip

◄ Grip
Use the eastern forehand grip, but with the racket face more open (i.e. facing towards the sky) than for a normal forehand.

Extra lift ►
To get the extra lift needed to play an effective lob you may have to lean back slightly as you play the shot.

3 Take the racket right back behind you so that you can hit the ball with a lot of swing. Start stepping forward with your leading foot.

4 Keeping your eyes fixed on the flight of the ball at all times, step forward towards it with your leading foot and swing the racket head at it.

5 Lift the racket from very low to high. Aim to hit the ball an arm's length from your body, slightly in front of you. Use your other hand to keep your balance.

Tactics

if you do lob the ball, then try to put it down your opponent's backhand side. Even if your lob is too low and your opponent plans to play a return smash, he is far more likely to miss a backhand smash than he is to miss a forehand smash.

Aim

Aim to lob the ball not too high and not too low. If you aim too low, your opponent will be able to reach it easily. If you aim too high he will have time to run back and return the ball after it has bounced. You should have a mental picture of how high your opponent's racket will be when stretched fully upwards, and aim to put the ball a few inches above this level.

THE FOREHAND LOB

Returning a lob

As soon as you realize that the ball is going up in the air for a lob, you have a split second to decide what to do. If you are tall you may want to jump up and try to reach it. The smash is the ideal return. But be ready to run to the back of the court if the ball goes above your reach. If you are a shorter player you should immediately sprint to the back of the court and play a groundstroke after the ball has bounced. It is often a good idea to reply to a lob with another lob, because your opponent may have run to the net when he sees you retreat to the back of the court.

6 Follow right up and through the direction of the ball, lifting it upward, over your opponent's head.

7 A full follow-through means the ball will stay on the strings of your racket for as long as possible and you'll be able to send it over your opponent's head and out of reach.

Topspin

If you are able to impart topspin on to the ball during the lob, then you'll find that when it lands in your opponent's court it will bounce high and away, right to the back of the court, so that even if your opponent chases the ball as soon as he or she realizes you're lobbing, it will still be out of reach.

◀ Practice

A common problem with the lob is that players either fail to put the ball high enough into the air, and end up feeding it to their opponent for an easy smash, or else they put too much pace on it and send the ball out beyond their opponent's baseline. Practise strengthening your lob by setting up cones (or sweaters) as markers along the opposite baseline and aim to hit in between them with a strong lob from your side of the court.

THE FOREHAND SMASH

The smash is a powerful shot that is hit from high to low without allowing the ball to bounce.

Any time that you are given the opportunity to do a forehand smash you should see it as a free point. The opportunity often arises after your opponent has sent you a lob, a shot which travels from low to high. You should hit the ball very hard, in the centre of the racket face, and aim into the furthest corner of the court.

Make sure you are totally confident about the shot or you will end up putting the ball either into the net or out beyond the court boundary. If you're not totally confident then run back behind the ball, allow it to bounce, and play a groundstroke.

You should practise your smash so that it becomes a formidable shot in your repertoire, and any time your opponent puts a ball high into the air you can win the point with a smash leaving your opponent helpless.

1 Start in the ready position, with knees bent, racket at waist height and head forward with your eyes on the ball.

2 Move quickly into a position underneath the falling ball. Instead of running backwards (if you have been lobbed), run sideways so that you keep your balance.

Grips ▶

Use the service, or "chopper" grip. Beginners may prefer to start smashing with an eastern forehand grip, but this should be modified to a "chopper" grip as confidence grows. Like the serve, it is hard to get the required power, speed or accuracy on a smash if you don't learn to use the "chopper" grip.

"Chopper" grip

Eastern forehand grip

THE FOREHAND SMASH

3 Keep your eye on your opponent's movements, anticipating the shot and the drop of the ball. Begin to take the racket back and up.

4 The racket should now be above your head and your body at full stretch.

5 Throw the racket head at the ball and aim to strike it when your body is at full stretch. Strike the ball with power. Keep a firm but flexible grip.

Position

If you have been lobbed and you reach up to the ball but it is just a bit too high for you to smash it properly, then run back quickly, wait for the ball to bounce and play a groundstroke. If your opponent has played a high ball with no topspin then the ball will bounce high and straight and will be easy to return. However, a looping topspin lob will bounce to the back of the court.

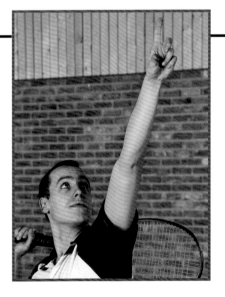

◀ A helping hand

If you point at the falling ball with your free hand during the forehand smash, it will help you focus on the ball and hit it accurately. The ball gathers speed as it falls, through the forces of gravity, and therefore it is hard to predict when to strike it. Your hand will act as a guide to judge the speed and distance of the ball.

Receiving position ▶

For either the forehand or backhand smash you have to get into position very quickly. Always sidestep backwards or forwards underneath the falling ball, rather than run, so that you don't lose your balance.

Facing a smash

As soon as you see your opponent getting ready to smash, you should try to anticipate where he is going to play the ball. This is often impossible to do because the ball travels so fast after it has been smashed. The safest position is behind the baseline, in the middle of the court, near the centre mark, as the power of a smashed ball will usually propel it to the furthest parts of the court.

If you are able to reach the smash it is unlikely that you will have much time to do anything but block it and hope it goes back into your opponent's court.

Advanced players will try to return a smash with a lob, because the opponent is at the net, but this is very hard to do.

6 Follow through in the direction of the ball, curling your wrist slightly forwards so that the ball doesn't land beyond the back of your opponent's court.

7 Bring the racket head down and to the other side of your body and then immediately get ready to play the next shot.

To smash or not?

It is easy and very embarrassing to fail to hit a smash. Even professionals do it, and it can be so disheartening that it puts you off your game for the next few points. You've got to be sure that you can make the smash and put it into your opponent's court before you decide to go through with the shot. If in doubt, sprint to the back of the court and play a groundstroke. You should smash only if you know you are going to have time to get yourself into the correct position under the ball, and you are fairly close to the net. Otherwise you'll miss the shot. If you're not sure that you'll make an effective smash then wait for the ball to bounce first and play an ordinary groundstroke.

Remember that if your opponent anticipates your smash it will lose its impact, so don't make your strategy too obvious.

THE BACKHAND SMASH

The backhand smash is a similar shot to the forehand smash, but played across the body with the backhand. Again, it is a powerful high to low shot, where the ball does not bounce.

The backhand smash is one of the trickiest shots in tennis. Thankfully the opportunity to play it rarely occurs. However, you should still practise it, as those rare opportunities may just win you the game.

The backhand smash shot will feel very unnatural to play as you are combining the complications of the backhand with a dangerous overhead ball. If you are not completely confident of smashing the ball correctly then, as with the forehand smash, sprint to the back of the court, allow the ball to bounce and get ready to play a forehand or backhand groundstroke. Alternatively, try letting the ball drop slightly further through the air until it's at the side of your body and then play a volley from the middle of the court.

1 Always start in the ready position, with knees slightly bent, head forward and racket at waist height. You should be ready to move to either side very quickly.

2 Start bringing the racket back in a smooth arc as soon as you realize the ball is coming in high and to your backhand. Begin to twist your body round slightly.

Position

When you are ready to strike the ball, you should be positioned so that the ball is slightly in front of you and on the backhand side. You will need very nimble footwork to get into this position.

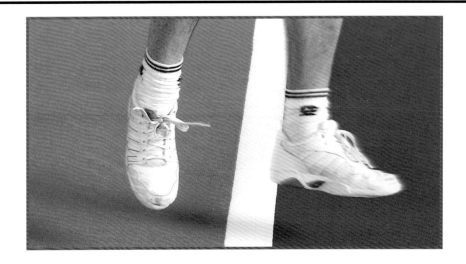

3 If you need to move back then sidestep backwards rather than run. The racket should be drawn back as far as you can, for power, with the elbow pointing upwards.

4 As you bring the racket up to meet the ball, your body should now be side-on to the net. Keep this position as you strike and follow through.

5 Strike the ball hard in the centre of the racket with your body stretched to maximum height. Use your non-hitting arm to keep your balance.

◄ Height

Some players like to give themselves extra height when they play a smash by jumping off the ground as they strike the ball. The higher you are off the ground, the more of your opponent's court you have to aim for. The extra height will also give you more power to bring the racket down hard over the ball.

Grip ►

Use the backhand grip for this shot. You may find that you can generate the extra power needed for the backhand smash with the double-handed backhand grip. However, you will sacrifice the reach for the power.

Backhand grip

Safety

As with all overhead shots, take care when you are moving backwards. You will need to have your eyes on the ball to judge the speed and power of its decent, so don't look round as you run backwards. The safest way to move backwards is to make small steps sideways and slightly back, moving backwards gradually without loosing your balance.

THE BACKHAND SMASH

Facing a backhand smash

Because it is more natural for the arm to come across the front of the body on a backhand, the vast majority of backhand smashes will be played across court to your backhand (or your forehand if you're left-handed). Therefore, as soon as you realize your opponent is playing a backhand smash, get ready to block the ball on your backhand side.

Don't make it too obvious to your opponent that you plan to cover this side because otherwise he may try to put the ball down the line on your other side.

6 As you bring the racket down, your wrist should curl over slightly so that the racket face comes over the ball and hits it down into your opponent's court.

7 A full follow-through will mean the ball continues on its chosen trajectory. Get into the receiving position immediately, ready for the next shot.

Where to aim

If you find that you get an easy opportunity for a backhand smash, then hit the ball hard into your opponent's court, so that it bounces up high beyond his reach, into the back netting behind the court. Make sure that you don't hit the ball before it has passed the line of the net, and make sure you don't hit the net with your racket or you will lose the point.

◄ Positions

It is crucial to get yourself into the right position for the backhand smash. You should be standing sideways on to the ball. It is almost impossible to hit a backhand smash while facing the net.

Your position on the court is a matter for debate and should be adapted to the circumstances. Ideally you should be somewhere between the service line and the net. If you stand too far forward to the net you will find that when you hit the ball the racket will be too open, facing up towards the sky. If you stand too far back you will punch the ball into the net. You will need to estimate the trajectory and power of the ball before assuming the best position.

THE DROPSHOT

The dropshot is a shot played by nudging the ball just over the net so that your opponent fails to reach it before it bounces twice.

A good opportunity to play a dropshot is when your opponent is far back behind his own baseline. Put as much backspin on the ball as you can so that it bounces very short and very low, giving your opponent as little time as possible to reach the ball. The ideal dropshot will land well inside the service box, close to the net.

The dropshot is often used as a set-up shot, forcing your opponent to run close to the net and hit the ball up into the air. Your responding shot should be back to his baseline, or to volley his return, hopefully securing the point.

Dropshots are far more effective on slow surfaces like clay or shale, where the ball bounces much lower. On fast, hard courts it is much more difficult to stop the ball from bouncing higher and giving your opponent more time and opportunity to reach it.

1 Start in the ready position with your knees bent, your head forward and the racket at waist height.

2 Start taking the racket back as soon as you decide on the dropshot. Transfer your weight on to your back leg.

Grips ▶

For the dropshot use the normal eastern forehand grip (or the normal backhand grip if it's a backhand dropshot). Unlike the volley, where you use a punching motion, on the dropshot you should almost try to caress the ball over the net.

Eastern forehand grip

Backhand grip

THE DROPSHOT

3 After taking back the racket to half-way round your body, start stepping forward with your leading foot.

4 Keeping your eyes fixed on the flight of the ball at all times, step forward towards it with your leading foot and swing the racket head at it.

5 Bring the racket head right underneath the ball so as to slice it. You should aim to hit the ball an arm's length away from your body, slightly in front of you.

◀ Position

Make sure you really bend your knees so you can get right down to the level of the ball and impart an adequate slice. Use your non-playing hand to maintain balance.

Aim ▶

You want the ball to plop over the net without any pace, so you should play the shot with sensitivity rather than power. Be sure not to clip the net with your racket as you play a dropshot because this constitutes a foul shot.

Effective dropshots

Dropshots are most effective on slow surfaces like clay or shale. On hard courts it is difficult to stop the ball from bouncing high, so you have to make sure that your opponent is right at the back of the court, a long distance from where you plan to place the dropshot. When a dropshot lands it is normally travelling very slowly. If your opponent is able to reach it he will be able to return it very hard and fast, so be prepared.

6 Follow under and through in the direction of the ball so as to maximize the slice, and therefore the backspin, which will control and slow down the ball.

7 A full follow-through means the ball will stay on the strings of your racket for as long as possible and you'll be able to control its direction much more.

◄ Control the ball

Make sure the face of the racket is not too open (turned too far skyward) or the ball will travel high into the air and bounce up high when it lands, giving your opponent more of a chance of running forward and reaching it.

Tactics ►

If a dropshot is well played, your opponent won't be able to reach the ball, even if he sprints at top speed for it. He will be flustered and worn out for the next shot you play him.

STRATEGY

Tennis is not just a game of physical prowess: players need to use their brains if they want to win. It's not enough merely to play a good shot: in the few seconds that you have between shots, you have to think about the options open to you and then play exactly the right shot for that situation.

Consistency

Consistency is the key to success in tennis. If you are able to play at a consistent level, and take few chances, then you have a better hope of winning as your opponent may start to take risks and make mistakes.

Too many novice players try to hit the ball hard on every stroke, imitating the professional players, and end up making errors. It is often far better to play what is called "percentage tennis", which means you go for more basic shots that have a higher percentage chance of going in. At beginners' level,

▲ Don't lose your cool over false line calls. Getting flustered will put you off your game.

if you avoid risking difficult shots and wait for your opponent to make a mistake instead, you are more likely to win the game.

Dealing with cheats

In tennis many balls land on or very close to the lines. The furthest extremities of the court are often the areas that players will aim for, so as to move their opponent about as much as possible in the hopes of catching him off-guard. Occasionally you're going to come across a player who you think is making false line calls on purpose. What should you do?

- First, give your opponent the benefit of the doubt and don't jump to conclusions.
- Ask them calmly if they are sure the ball was out.
- Never accuse them of cheating.
- Never scream or shout at your opponent.
- If you're convinced they're cheating then you should challenge them and demand a let. If this doesn't work, ask for help from an official or a third party.
- The best option is to be determined to beat them by playing more skilfully than them.

The tiebreak

When a set reaches six games all, players have to play a tiebreak to determine who wins. Here are some

▲ Winning at tennis requires mental planning and strategic thinking.

tips on keeping your cool under these tense conditions:

- Make sure you are familiar with the scoring and serving system or you will get flustered and lose points.
- Play safe with your first serves. Don't try for aces every time: it is too risky at this stage of the set.
- Play aggressively, but not in such an extreme manner that you lose control and make errors.
- Pick on your opponent's weaknesses more than ever. Every point counts now, so if you know your opponent has a weak backhand, for example, then put pressure on it.
- Play one point at a time. If you're losing badly in a tiebreak, forget the preceding points and think only about the point in hand.
- Stay focused and calm. The tiebreak is usually brief and the player who can maintain concentration for the longest is often the winner.

▲ Tennis should be a fun and friendly game to be enjoyed whether you win or lose.

Dealing with adverse weather

Tennis is no longer the summertime sport it was once thought to be. Today people play all over the world in all seasons and therefore often have to put up with adverse weather conditions. If you're not lucky enough to have access to an indoor tennis court then sooner or later you are going to come across rain, strong winds, blinding sunlight, ice or even snow.

At the first sign of bad weather many players lose their concentration and blame their poor play on the elements. But remember, it's exactly the same for your opponent, so rather than complain, try to use the weather to your advantage.

Strong winds

Watch the ball very carefully before you hit it and be ready in case the wind blows it about at the last minute.

If the wind is at your back, you will have to be very careful not to put the ball beyond the back of your opponent's court. But if you are playing into the wind, you can take more risks and hit the ball harder without sending it too long. You can make good use of shots such as the dropshot and the lob because the wind will work to your advantage.

Make sure you take the wind into account when serving. If the wind is coming from the side, you may want to serve in the same direction so that the ball swings wide for your opponent. But if it is really windy you may have to resort to an underarm serve.

Rain

It is not advisable to play in heavy rain. In light rain the court gets slippery, the balls get heavy and the raindrops fall into your eyes when you serve. If you have to play, then make sure you have decent grips on the soles of your shoes and that you sweep the court between games. Try to force your opponent into frequent changes of direction as the slippery surface will slow him down. Lobs are ideal shots to play because when your opponent looks up to return them with a smash he will get raindrops in his eyes.

Snow and ice

Only play if you really have to. Wear shoes with good grips and sweep the court before playing. Keep the direction changing so as to wrong-foot your opponent. Make sure you wear warm but non-restrictive clothing.

Bright sunlight

Sunglasses or a peaked cap will help when you serve or smash into the sun. You may need to change your ball throw-up or the way you stand when you serve if the sun is really bright. Try to lob your opponent when you know he will be looking upwards into the sun.

Preparing for matches

If you are getting ready to play a match, remember the following advice:

- Eat well the night before. Make sure you consume plenty of carbo-hydrates such as pasta and potatoes.
- Get lots of sleep.
- Eat a substantial meal and drink plenty of fluids before the match. Do not eat a large meal up to two hours before you are due to play.
- Remember to bring everything you need in your kitbag: at least two rackets, shoes, socks, shorts or skirt, shirt, tracksuit, sweatband, headwear, balls, food for after the match, plenty of water, plasters (Band-Aids), suncream etc.
- Arrive at the court well before your match is due to start. If you are late you will be flustered. If you're playing doubles, then make sure you agree to meet your partner well before the match starts so you can discuss tactics.
- Stretch fully and warm up your muscles before you play.
- Make sure you play a proper pre-match warm-up with your opponent before starting the match.

SINGLES STRATEGY

Singles is a much tougher, much more competitive sport than doubles. You are playing over a large area, so you have to think, run and recover quickly.

The winner is often simply the fittest player who manages to keep the ball in play for a longer time. Stamina and endurance are essential qualities.

Serve and volley

On fast surfaces such as hard, artificial grass and real grass courts, you should aim to play close to the net if you hit a strong first service. This is called "serve-and-volley". This way you may be able to control the net play and keep your opponent on the baseline where he is more likely to send the ball into the net. However, many successful players rarely approach the net and are able to dominate the court from the baseline with powerful groundstrokes.

Serving position

When you serve in singles, try to stand as close to the centre of the baseline as possible, so that, whether you rush the net or not, you're still able to control the court from a central position. You

▲ When playing singles, you need to be fit and have the power to sustain long, hard rallies.

▲ Stand close to the baseline when serving.

will be in a good position to run either way when your opponent hits his return. If you leave a gap either side of the court, your opponent will exploit it.

Placing shots

Practise altering the angle of the racket head as you hit the ball so that when you play your shots you can place them into an uncovered area of your opponent's court.

Often, a slow but controlled shot into an unexpected area of the court is far more effective than a powerful bullet that blasts across the net but lands close to your adversary. As a general rule, balls that you hit flat and hard will travel in a straight line, whereas if you hit balls more softly, or with spin, you'll be able to create more angles.

Try hitting the ball in different, unexpected directions. If your opponent is on the right-hand side of the court, hit the ball down the left-hand side. Keep him running around after the ball and tire him out. Also try changing the pace of the game. If you are both hitting strong baseline groundstrokes to each other, then it might really throw your opponent if you suddenly hit a dropshot. Variety is often the key to success.

Temper control

Because singles is an individual sport, and you can't blame lost points on a partner as you can in doubles, it is always very easy to get angry with yourself for playing bad shots. If you want to stay on top of the game you must learn to control your temper and keep a cool head.

Sometimes tennis can be the most infuriating sport in the world, but if you don't maintain your mental discipline on court you run the risk of losing every point out of sheer frustration. Your opponent will sense your confusion and take advantage.

▲ Place your shots so that you confuse your opponent. Don't let him feel that he knows your game so well that there are no surprises and he can predict your shots.

▲ Don't let the frustrations of a hard game let you become a bad sport. It should be fun!

DOUBLES STRATEGY

Remember that doubles tennis is a team sport. You're no longer out there, fending for yourself. Now you've got a partner to worry about, too.

Move in unison

Many coaches say that the most successful doubles teams are those that move in unison. When one partner rushes the net, so does the other. One runs back for a lob and so does the other, and in doubles, one thing is for sure, you have to attack at the net.

Where to stand

When you serve in doubles stand slightly away from the centre of the baseline so that, when you run towards the net after the serve (which you should always do when your serve is strong enough), you are able to control both your side of the court and your tramline (doubles court). Run in and try to volley your opponent's return of serve back to his side of the court.

If your partner is serving then you should stand on your side of the court, in the service box, two metres (just over six feet) from the net. You should be ready to block your opponent's return of serve down the middle of the court and you should under no circumstances ever let your opponent put the ball back down your tramlines (doubles court). Points lost down the net player's tramlines (doubles court) are unforgivable.

When you're returning serve in doubles, ideally you should aim to put

▲ If you work with your partner, not against him, you will stand a much better chance of winning the game. A successful doubles partnership is based on understanding each other's strategy.

▲ Plan your positions with your partner before the game. It will really pay off.

the ball right back at the feet of the incoming server. Never play the ball at the other opponent covering the net unless he's a weak net player or he's left a gap down the tramlines (doubles court). Always take care not to aim directly at the body of your opponent or you could seriously injure him. When your partner is returning the serve you should stand on your side of the court, on the service-box line, ready to move to the net or the baseline if you need to. Advanced players will stand nearer the net, while weaker players might stand behind the baseline. Whatever you do, don't get caught in no man's land – the area between the baseline position at the back of the court and the volleying position close to the net.

Communicate with your partner

Because you're in a team it's crucial to communicate with your partner. Call for the ball as soon as you can, to let your partner know early that you are taking it. There is nothing more embarrassing than when both players assume that their partner will take the ball, and it bounces down the middle of the court, right between the two of you. Likewise, don't end up in a collision as you both go for the ball.

Professional doubles players often talk to each other before every point, or the net player will use signs to tell the server that he plans to do a special move. You should communicate with and encourage your partner constantly.

▲ Communication is an essential quality in doubles partnerships. Let your partner know which balls you intend to take. Don't assume that the ball is yours or you could end up in a collision.

DOUBLES STRATEGY

Picking on one player

In doubles, and especially mixed doubles, players are often tempted to repeatedly hit the ball straight back to the weaker player in the hope that he or she will become tired and make an error. Although this is a good idea in competitive tennis, in social tennis it is not acceptable and your opponents will have every right to complain that you are being unsportsmanlike if you persist in this manner.

▲ Working in harmony with your partner will increase the speed and enjoyment of the game.

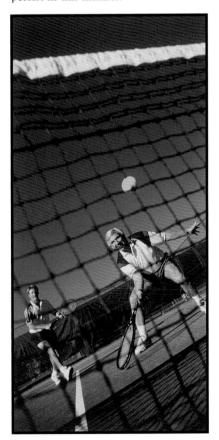

▲ Doubles should be dynamic and exciting.

Which side should you play?

It's a good idea to get used to playing on a particular side in doubles, especially if you have a regular partner.

As a very basic rule, right-handed players with a stronger backhand should play on the left, while right-handers with a stronger forehand should play on the right. If a "leftie" and a "rightie" are playing together they might want to put the leftie on the left to go for the wide shots on the forehand, and the rightie on the right for the same reason. However, there is no hard-and-fast rule. Do whatever feels right and gets the best results.

ADAPTING TO DIFFERENT SURFACES

Different surfaces affect how hard and fast the ball bounces and how quickly you can move around the court. You may not always be able to play on your preferred surface, so you should develop a variety of strategies to suit the surface you are playing on.

Hard courts

The great thing about hard courts is that, unless they are the cracked tarmac ones so often found in local parks, the bounce is almost always

▲ Clay courts will slow down the ball.

▲ Grass is a fast surface and is gentler on your knee and ankle joints than hard courts.

true. To play well you will have to vary your serve much more, hit your volleys much deeper and generally try to keep your groundstrokes low on the ground. However be warned – playing frequently on hard courts can cause injury to your ankle and knee joints, which can be very painful. Make sure you warm up adequately, have suitable shoes with padding in the toe and ankle to reduce the harsh impact, and wear a knee support.

Grass courts

Because grass is a much faster surface than some of the others, it favours the serve-and-volleyer. Baseline players are prevented from attacking serves well because the bounce is low and resists a powerful return. The servers who run into the net and kill the ball are almost always the ones who win on grass. Grass courts are soft, and are therefore less harsh on your ankle and knees.

ADAPTING TO DIFFERENT SURFACES

Clay or shale courts

Clay or shale courts are slower than other courts, and therefore they favour baseline players who thrive on long, drawn-out rallies. Dropshots are particularly effective on clay courts because your opponent will almost certainly be at the baseline and because, with the right spin, the ball will bounce much lower and softer than on other surfaces. Fitter players often have an advantage on clay or shale courts because they are able to survive the long rallies and don't get exhausted running backwards and forward along the baseline as they covering all different parts of the court.

▲ Hard courts with a decent, maintained surface enable a true bounce.

Other surfaces

Artificial grass is becoming a very popular alternative surface. When brand-new it has a good grip, like firm clay, and favours the baseliner. But over time, as the plastic blades become flattened, it gets much slicker and smoother and favours the serve-and-volleyer. If you fall over on artificial grass it can burn your skin badly and can be extremely painful.

Carpet courts have become very popular recently, and they offer a really sure grip for your feet, but many clubs insist that you wear special indoor shoes to protect the surface.

▲ Indoor courts with carpet surfaces are becoming popular. You may need to wear special shoes.

RULES AND SCORING

The scoring system

Players should agree before they start how many sets their match will consist of. To win a set you need to win six games before your opponent does with a margin of at least two games. To save time, most amateur players will play a tiebreak when they reach six games all, except in the final set of a match, when they continue until one player has reached a two-game lead.

To win a game you need to win four points before your opponent does, with a margin of at least two points. Until a player wins a point his score is called "love" which means nil. The server's score is always called first. The first point you win gives you a score of 15, the second gives you 30, the third gives you 40 and the fourth wins you the game. If both players reach 40, the score is called deuce and either player must win one point, called advantage, and then immediately the next point, which wins the game. If he fails to win the next point the score reverts to deuce again.

Players must change ends when the number of games played reaches an odd number, to equalize any natural advantages the court may have.

Choices at the start

Before you start the game, flip a coin to decide who starts serving. If you win the toss you can choose to serve, choose to receive, choose to start at a certain end or ask your opponent to make the choice.

▲ Touching the net with your body or clothing will lose you a point.

RULES AND SCORING

Where to stand

At the beginning of each game you stand behind the baseline on the right-hand side of the baseline if you are serving. You then have two chances to hit the ball diagonally into the left-hand service box on the other side of the net. If the ball skims the net before it lands in the correct service box, a let is played. From then on the server alternates between the left-and the right-hand service boxes after every point until the game has been won. If either player fails to return the ball before it has bounced more than once within the boundary of their opponent's court then they lose the point. In doubles you are allowd to hit the ball into the tramlines (doubles court) along both sides of the court.

The tiebreak

When the score reaches six-all in a set, the player whose turn it is to serve begins the tiebreak. He serves just one point to the normal side. Then his opponent serves two points starting from the wrong side. Players subsequently change serves every two points and change ends after every six points. The tiebreak is won by the first player to reach seven points (with a margin of at least two points). In doubles the tiebreak serving order is the same as the normal serving order.

Most players do not play a tiebreak in the final set of a match – they wait until one player is two games ahead. But you must agree this rule before you start the match.

▲ Flip a coin to decide who serves first and which end you play from.

On-court etiquette

Individual tennis clubs will have different rules of etiquette. Here are some basic points which you should abide by at all times, as a matter of courtesy to your fellow players:

• Do not scream, shout, or make unnecessary noises when you are on the court. You could ruin other players' concentration and make them miss a point which is extremely annoying.
• Never walk on to a court when a point is in progress. You will disrupt the game and may get injured by a

flying ball. Wait until the point is decided before you cross. The safest way to cross a court is to keep right back near the rear netting.

• Try to prevent your balls from rolling on to other courts. If you must retrieve them, do so between points, quickly and quietly, without disrupting the other game.

• Return any stray balls from other courts as soon as possible. If you accidentally stand on a stray ball, it can be very dangerous.

• Never throw balls around the court, or throw your racket into the net.

• Do not lean against the net or you will cause it to slacken.

The rules and scoring system in tennis can seem rather daunting to a beginner, but it is quite straightforward and you will soon get the hang of it.

Essential rules

• When you serve, your foot must not touch the baseline or the inside of the court before you strike the ball. Contrary to popular belief, you are allowed to serve overarm, or underarm if you prefer.

• Whenever you strike the ball you must hit it only once. However, unintentional double hits are permitted during a rally.

• You lose the point if you touch the net with your body, racket or clothing while the ball is still in play.

• The only time you are allowed to lean over the line of the net and hit the ball is when your opponent has put so much backspin on the ball or the wind

is so strong that the ball goes back to your opponent's side of the net before it bounces twice.

• If you play the ball and it hits another ball lying in the court, your opponent must still make a valid return. Your opponent will still try to hit it, even if it bounces wildly.

• If the ball lands on the boundary of the court it is called "in". If one player is not sure, it is still considered good. Always give the benefit of the doubt to your opponent and resist getting into heated arguments.

• If the ball hits the net posts or singles sticks and then lands in the correct court, the shot is still good.

▲ Watch out for foot faults. You must not let your feet touch the baseline during a serve.

▲ Keep well back from the baseline during the serve or you will lose the point.

GLOSSARY

Ace
A winning serve that is hit into the correct service box so powerfully that your opponent fails to touch it.

Advantage
After the score reaches deuce (i.e. 40–40) the next point won is called an advantage.

Advantage court
When serving, the advantage court is the right hand half of your opponent's court, where you would be serving to if either of you held an advantage.

Approach shot
A shot played before a player attacks the net.

ATP
The Association of Tennis Professionals. The body set up to govern men's professional tennis across the world.

Backhand
A shot played with the back of your hand facing the ball (i.e. on the left-hand side of your body if you're right-handed, or the right hand side if you're left-handed).

Backspin
Backspin is spin played by positioning the racket underneath the ball as you hit it, making the ball spin backwards with a short bounce after landing.

Ball boy and ball girl
Young helpers in professional tournaments, who collect stray balls in between services and points.

Ball machine
A device which shoots balls out of a tube at speed and allows players to practise tennis without an opponent.

Baseline
The line marking the rear boundary of the court.

Centre mark
The short line that bisects the middle of the baseline.

"Chopper" grip
A way of holding the racket. Also called the service grip.

Closed racket face
When the racket is angled downwards, towards the ground.

Cross-court
A shot played diagonally across the tennis court.

Deuce
When the score reaches 40–40 (i.e. both players have won three points each) it is called "deuce". The term comes from the French word *deux* meaning two.

Deuce court
As you are facing your opponent, the deuce court is the left hand half of his court where you would be serving to if the score was deuce.

Double fault
If both first and second serves fail to go in, it is called a "double fault" and you lose the point.

Doubles
Tennis between two teams of two players.

Down the line
A shot played down one side of the court rather than diagonally across it.

Drop shot
A shot that lands close to the net and bounces short and low.

Eastern grip
The grip used to play a basic forehand.

Fault
A serve that fails to go in.

Follow through
The action of the racket after the shot has been made.

Foot fault
When your foot touches the baseline or the inside of the court before you strike the serve. A foot fault will lose you a point.

Forehand
A shot played with the front of your hand facing the ball.

Game
A new player starts serving at the beginning of each game. When one player has won four points and is at least two points ahead of his opponent, he wins the game.

Grand Slam
A name given to any one of the four most important tennis tournaments in the world. These are: Wimbledon in London, England; the US Open in New York, USA; the French Open in Paris, France; and the Australian Open in Melbourne, Australia.

Groundstroke
A shot played after the ball has bounced.

Half-volley
A shot played just after the ball has bounced.

ITF
The International Tennis Federation. The body in charge of international tennis throughout the world.

Leading foot
The foot that you step forward with towards the ball before hitting it.

Let
When the point is played over again. If players are unsure whether the ball was in or out, or if a player is unfairly distracted, then a let should be played. Similarly, if a service goes in but clips the net first, then a let is played.

Linesperson
At major tournaments a linesperson is employed to judge whether balls land in or out of court.

Lob
A shot played high up over your opponent's head.

Love
In tennis, if the score is nil then it is called "love". This term is thought to have come from the French word *l'oeuf*, meaning egg, because an egg is the same shape as a zero.

Love game
A game where one player (or doubles team) fails to score a single point.

Match
A match is a competitive game of tennis which consists of a prearranged number of sets (normally three or five).

Match point
When a player needs just one more point to win the match.

Mixed doubles
Doubles between two teams of one male and one female player.

Open racket face
When the racket is angled upwards.

Passing shot
A shot that passes above the net while you are standing at the net.

GLOSSARY

Poaching
When a player in a doubles team cuts across and takes his partner's shot. This is a serious breach of etiquette.

Rally
A sequence of shots played between players without a break, either in a match or when practising.

Receiving position
The position in which the player stands in ready to receive a shot. The feet should be spread shoulder-width apart, the knees slightly bent, with the body weight positioned on the balls of the feet. The racket should be raised to shoulder height.

Referee
At major tournaments the overall officiator.

Seeds
The rank given to players in major competitions. The purpose of seeding is to prevent the top players eliminating each other in the early stages of a tournament.

Semi-western grip
The grip used to hit high-bouncing balls with a lot of topspin.

Serve-and-volley
Playing a volley close to the net straight after a service.

Service
Every point starts with the server playing a serve from behind his baseline into the opposite service box.

Service box
The areas of the court which the serve must land in order to win a point.

Set
The first player to win six games wins the set (provided he is at least two games ahead of his opponent).

Set point
When a player needs just one more point to win the set.

Sidelines or tramlines (doubles court)
The two strips running alongside the edge of a singles court are called sidelines or tramlines (doubles court). They are only used for doubles play. Balls hit into this area are deemed out in the singles game.

Sidespin
Similar to the backspin, but the racket

comes up underneath the side of the ball as it hit it.

Singles
A game of tennis played by two players.

Singles sticks
Used to prop up each end of the net at a point 0.91 metres (3 feet) from the edge of the singles court. For doubles

play the singles sticks are removed so that players can play shots down the sidelines (doubles court) more easily.

Slice
A shot played using backspin or sidespin.

Smash
A high ball struck above the head which drops low over the net. The smash is played with power.

Stop volley
A volley which drastically reduces the speed of the ball and causes it to drop short into your opponent's court.

String savers
Small pieces of plastic inserted at the point where the racket strings cross. They prevent your strings from rubbing against one another and wearing thin.

Sweet-spot
The small area around the centre of the racket strings from which a good shot is normally struck.

Tennis elbow
A painful affliction in the elbow often caused by racket vibration, wrong-sized grip or poor grip technique.

Tiebreak
When the score reaches 6–6 in a set a tiebreak has to be played, except in the last set of a match. The first player who wins seven points, and is at least two points ahead of his opponent, wins the tiebreak and therefore the set.

Topspin
Spin caused when you bring the racket over the ball as you hit it, thereby causing it to spin forwards and bounce high and long after it lands.

Umpire
In major tournaments umpires will sit on raised chairs at the side of the court and preside over the matches, ensuring that the score is always correct and that the rules are adhered to. Their decision must be respected.

Unforced error
An error or lost point caused by your own mistake, rather than your opponent's good play, such as a ball out of court or a ball that goes into the net.

Vibration dampener
A small rubber device placed at the bottom of the racket's strings, used to prevent vibration when you hit the ball. It makes shots cleaner and can help prevent tennis elbow.

Volley
A shot played before the ball bounces. It is often played close to the net.

Western grip
A more extreme version of the semi-western grip, used to hit the ball with maximum topspin.

WTA
The Women's Tennis Association. The body set up to govern women's professional tennis across the world.

INDEX

ACKNOWLEDGEMENTS

The publisher would like to thank the following people for their contributions to this book:

Models
Charles Howgego
Jo Doherty

Feeder
Marcus Crowe

Thanks also to the Riverside Club, Northwood, Middlesex, UK, for the use of the court.

Picture Credits
t = top, b= bottom, l = left, r = right
Tony Stone Images: 6; 7; 11t; 12bl; 14bl; 71; 72l; 75t, b; 76; 77l, r; 78l, r; 79t; 80l, r; 83l; 91l; 92l, r; 96l.
Ace magazine © Gerard Brown: 25.

All other photographs
© Anness Publishing Ltd

Diagrams by John Hawkins

The following suppliers kindly lent equipment and clothing for photography:

Adidas UK Ltd: clothing and bag

Reebok UK Ltd: clothing

Fischer: rackets

Nike: tennis shoes and clothing

Penn: tennis balls